HONEST GOVERNMENT

Honest Government

AN ETHICS GUIDE FOR PUBLIC SERVICE

W. J. Michael Cody and
Richardson R. Lynn

FOREWORD BY
Senator Howard Baker

PRAEGER

Westport, Connecticut
London

Library of Congress Cataloging-in-Publication Data

Cody, W. J. Michael.
    Honest government : an ethics guide for public service / W. J.
  Michael Cody and Richardson R. Lynn ; foreword by Senator Howard
  Baker.
      p.   cm.
    Includes bibliographical references and index.
    ISBN 0–275–94178–7 (alk. paper). — ISBN 0–275–94376–3 (pbk.)
    1. Political ethics—United States.   I. Lynn, Richardson R.
  II. Title.
  JK468.E7C63   1992
  172′.0973—dc20   92–7480

British Library Cataloguing in Publication Data is available.

Library of Congress Catalog Card Number: 92–7480
ISBN: 0–275–94178–7
      0–275–94376–3 (pbk.)

First published in 1992

Praeger Publishers, 88 Post Road West, Westport, CT 06881
An imprint of Greenwood Publishing Group, Inc.

Printed in the United States of America

The paper used in this book complies with the
Permanent Paper Standard issued by the National
Information Standards Organization (Z39.48–1984).

10 9 8 7 6 5 4 3 2 1

To Lucius E. Burch, Jr., Jameson M. Jones, and my father, Jim Cody—for trying to teach me what was right.

—W. J. M. C.

To David F. Lynn, an ethical public servant and a great brother.

—R. R. L.

Contents

Contents

Foreword

From Watergate in the 1970s to the savings and loan scandals of today, the American people have grown more and more suspicious of their own elected representatives, erecting more and more elaborate—and ill-conceived—structures to police public ethics, driving more and more talented men and women away from the public service arena for fear they cannot meet the standard of perfection our society now seems to insist upon.

Having investigated many of these scandals myself, and having helped shape the institutional reforms that flowed from those investigations, I know better than most that we still have not developed a very useful code of official conduct to help our political leaders stay out of trouble. I also doubt that a truly comprehensive code, showing how to deal with every temptation the politician is heir to, will ever be written, or that the truly honorable politician really needs one.

Nevertheless, I believe Michael Cody and Richardson Lynn have performed a tremendous public service with the publication of the book you now hold. *Honest Government: An Ethics Guide for Public Service* comes as close as mortals are likely to come to a commonsense guide to acceptable political conduct, and I commend Messrs. Cody and Lynn both for undertaking this important work and for doing it so well.

One book may not turn the tide, but *Honest Government* is an awfully good start.

—Senator Howard Baker

Preface

This book grows out of a personal interest in the ethics of public service that began in school. Let me briefly describe my background, not because it makes me an expert in government ethics, but because it may explain my perspective and strong convictions. My religious beliefs played a major role in pushing me toward politics. The Presbyterian influence on me as a young person emphasized the value of a life of service. At Southwestern at Memphis (now Rhodes College), I considered studying for the ministry but gradually came to see the same potential for service in public life. Those were relatively innocent days, before the turmoil of the 1960s, the cynicism of the 1970s, and the selfish bungling of the 1980s. In college, I wrote a senior paper titled "An Ethical Politician?" I have spent a substantial part of my adult life trying to answer that question.

After serving in student leadership roles in school, church, and college, I decided to attend law school with the notion that a legal background was useful preparation for public service. I worked in the Memphis mayoral campaign of Edmund Orgill and a reelection campaign of U.S. Senator Estes Kefauver. I attended the University of Virginia School of Law in the heady days of the New Frontier, under the spell of John F. Kennedy's dynamic invitation for young people to enter public service, either here or overseas in the Peace Corps. His message of unselfish service to others was essentially the same as the message of the Presbyterian church that had motivated me during my early years.

I did well in law school and was actively recruited by law firms in Philadelphia and Washington, D.C. However, Memphis attorney Lucius E. Burch, Jr., convinced me that I should return to Memphis, where I could make a more significant contribution to the community. He argued that a lawyer had an obligation to do more than making a living—that he should be of service to society in a broader sense. Memphis and the South generally were entering a risky period of transition in relations between the races during the mid–1960s. I didn't need much convincing. I came home.

After helping to coordinate President Kennedy's 1960 campaign on the Virginia state campuses, I returned to Memphis, Tennessee, and Southern politics. In 1969, I helped found the L. Q. C. Lamar Society, a group that attempted to provide some direction for a rapidly changing and developing South. Through that work, I met a quietly impressive Georgia politician, Jimmy Carter. The Lamar Society was transformed into the Southern Growth Policies Board, a nonpartisan, multistate agency for which Senator Terry Sanford, then President of Duke University, arranged funding from the legislatures of the Southern states. Back in Memphis, I became Chairman of the Shelby County Democratic Party and was elected an at-large member of the City Council. I was especially proud that my support in the council race cut across the class and racial boundaries that seemed to divide Memphis on many issues and allowed me to carry almost every box in the city.

I served on the National Steering Committee for presidential candidate Carter and headed his effort in western Tennessee. President Carter appointed me U.S. Attorney for the Western District of Tennessee. In addition to exposing me to an entirely new role in government, my office prosecuted politicians and public officials during the post-Watergate era when under-the-table practices of long standing became the focus of federal investigation and enforcement. My interest in ethics also helped me keep one foot in academia: I was an Adjunct Professor of Professional Ethics at the Memphis State University School of Law.

After completing my term as U.S. Attorney, I ran for Mayor of Memphis. I lost, in part, because the racially diverse support I expected disappeared. The times had changed since my council race, and the Memphis vote reflected almost complete racial polarization.

The Justices of the Tennessee Supreme Court then appointed me Attorney General for the State of Tennessee. In that position, I saw new aspects of the same ethical dilemmas that I had experienced in the earlier roles of party chairman, municipal legislator, mayoral candidate, and U.S. Attorney. It gave me yet another perspective on the difficult choices that public officials must make in the conduct of their jobs. I resigned from the Attorney General's post in September 1988 to return to the private practice of law. I had always promised I would not borrow money in order to survive as a public official and, after exhausting my savings, decided to retire from public service.

My co-author, Richard Lynn, has not served in government, but he has taught in both law schools and graduate business schools since graduating from the Vanderbilt University School of Law. He served as Professor of Business Law and Ethics in the Jack C. Massey Graduate School of Business at Belmont College before returning to teach at the Pepperdine University School of Law. His years of teaching and writing about legal and business ethics provide a context for the ideas in this book that my experiences, by themselves, could not supply.

We want to thank the friends who reviewed earlier drafts of this book: Michael Catalano, Andrew Bennett, Robert Cooper, Jr., Dean Ronald F. Phillips of the Pepperdine University Law School, Liza Karsai for her invaluable last-minute help with the book, and Wayne Brown, who put Richard and me together for this project and strongly supported it. Finally, our friends and family deserve thanks for suffering our long silences and distracted looks while we put our ideas into final form.

—W. J. Michael Cody

Introduction

Americans deserve honest government. Public officials should be honest. Unfortunately, those platitudes are not useful as ethical guidelines because much of what public officials do falls into ethically gray areas. We expect that the most obvious graft or corruption will be punished if discovered. This book is not about reforming laws, although reform is needed. Rather, how do we measure the routine, day-to-day ethics of men and women who are in public service? We need a comprehensive statement of ethical behavior for public officials and employees at every level of government.

All public servants should read this book, but we especially hope it will be read by ordinary citizens. Too many people have a jaded, unrealistic impression that public servants are lazy, bloated bureaucrats, if not actually on the take. The resulting cynicism is reflected in low voter turnout, less-qualified candidates running for public office, and little public support for measures to make public service jobs attractive to the best-qualified men and women. Although we have used numerous examples to the contrary in this book, the conduct of our public officials is overwhelmingly honest and competent. Nor do we intend to accuse anyone who is specifically named of unethical conduct. Frequently, those examples are of well-meaning public servants who deserve better ethical guidance than they currently receive.

Public service ethics have already been addressed to some extent by federal, state, and local legislation. Typically, those laws only deal with campaign finance or conflicts of interest. Harvard Professor Dennis F. Thompson describes those laws as "minimalist ethics."[1] Many of the suggestions in this book should be implemented by legislation. But we are not primarily concerned with legislating ethics, even if that could be done. Rather, we hope to make a case for reasonable statements of duties owed by public officials to citizens and to the government itself.

The ultimate barrier to widespread adherence to high standards of public ethics is the feeling that it is a sign of weakness to insist on high standards or point out unethical conduct by others. If one candidate complains about the unfair tactics of an opponent, the public is likely to think that the candidate is whining or that it is the desperate cry of a losing candidate. How often do voters turn out an unethical but effective politician? Real men may not eat quiche, but real public servants can be both ethical and effective.

Finally, we both confess discomfort in writing about ethics. We are far from perfect and must struggle with ethical questions on a daily basis. While this book does not contain complete answers about the ethics of public officials, it identifies situations in which those officials ought to act cautiously and suggests high standards by which the people can measure the conduct of their public servants.

We hope that this book assists the ongoing discussion of public service ethics. There should be more debate about proper ethical standards and their enforcement. Citizens at every level of government must become involved in creating and monitoring the ethical rules that public servants will obey.

—Richardson R. Lynn

NOTE

1. D. Thompson, POLITICAL ETHICS AND PUBLIC OFFICE (1987).

HONEST GOVERNMENT

A Philosophy of Public Service

No discussion of public service ethics takes place in a vacuum. The post-Watergate emphasis on legal ethics continues and has been joined by the insider-trading spotlight on business ethics and the misadventures of several religious media stars. Despite the seeming wave of unethical conduct, there is no evidence that our moral standards have declined over the last few years, even in politics. Americans have always had a healthy skepticism about politicians, reflected in an old saying: "Don't tell my mother I'm a politician. She thinks I play piano in a whorehouse."

The increased attention to political ethics in the 1990s demonstrates a heightened sensitivity that leads to greater publicity and more efforts at reform. We are becoming more aware of the importance of public ethical standards. The philosopher Claes G. Ryn said, "What is absolute in man's ethical life . . . is not this or that standard of conduct which he formulates in response to the ethical demand on him, but the moral obligation itself, the imperative of always *looking* for the self-justifying solution in the particular situation."[1]

During the first few weeks of his presidency, George Bush made a concerted effort to sensitize federal officials to ethical concerns. At first this attempt seemed to backfire, because the increased scrutiny revealed ethical gaffes that were routinely ignored in prior administrations. One news story began, "President Bush's much vaunted ethics kick has turned into an ethics nightmare, and Democrats are enjoying the spectacle."[2]

Secretary of State James Baker was pressured to sell all publicly traded stock that he and his family owned, even though it was held in a blind trust. Stories about Senator John Tower's ethics and morality in public and private life plagued his unsuccessful quest to be Secretary of Defense. It was learned that the Secretary for Health and Human Services was negotiating for leave-of-absence pay from his employer while serving in government. And the President's chief ethics official, White House Counsel C. Boyden Gray, wisely resigned as chairman of a family-owned radio and cable television company and put his assets in a blind trust, even though he was not legally obligated to do either.

The lesson for President Bush and other conscientious officials is that those with the highest standards may receive the greatest criticism. Democrats could not enjoy the spectacle without hypocrisy, because the Democrats control Congress and numerous statehouses, institutions that have been less ethically aware than the Bush administration. For example, Governor Mario Cuomo created the New York State Commission on Governmental Integrity in 1987 under the authority given to him by the legislature. However, the legislature provided funding for the commission only on the condition that the commission use none of the funds for investigating the management or affairs of the legislature.

None of the ethical issues raised in this book are partisan issues. Any variety of misconduct can be found in either party. And pressure for real reform must come from both parties.

President Bush appointed eight distinguished men and women to the Commission on Federal Ethics Law Reform. The commission completed its report in March 1989. The report set the tone for this book when it stated

Ethical government means much more than laws. It is a spirit, an imbued code of conduct, an ethos. It is a climate in which, from the highest to the lowest ranks of policy- and decision-making officials, some conduct is instinctively sensed as correct and other conduct as being beyond acceptance.

Laws and rules can never be fully descriptive of what an ethical person should do. They can simply establish minimal standards of conduct. Possible variations in conduct are infinite, virtually impossible to describe and proscribe by statute. Compulsion by law is the most expensive way to make people behave.

The futility of relying solely or principally on compulsion to produce virtue becomes even more apparent when one considers that there is an obligation in a public official to be sure his actions appear ethical as well as be ethical.[3]

On April 12, 1989, President Bush signed Executive Order No. 12674, setting forth principles of ethical conduct for government officers and employees. Those principles could easily be applied to the other two branches of government and state governments as well.

GENERAL RULES

Regardless of whether society's overall moral bill of health is improving, more improvement is needed. In the field of public service ethics, there are numerous examples of failure and deceit. Simply organizing a laundry list of ways in which public officials have breached the public trust suggests the rules that ought to be followed.

Item—Defense Department official bribed to release confidential information.

Rule—Public officials should not take bribes.

Item—Judge hires incompetent brother-in-law as court officer.

Rule—Nepotism of any kind is improper.

The list could be lengthy. A major problem with any discussion of public service ethics is the lack of a standard, a widely accepted statement of what those ethics should be. Public servants are left with the rule that Vanderbilt Law School Professor Paul Hartman says sufficed to explain legal ethics when he was a law student in the 1930s: "Always follow your conscience, but first make sure you don't have the conscience of an ass." A few public officials practice the first part of that rule without conducting the self-examination required by the second part. In 1977, the Tennessee Senate adopted as part of its Code of Ethics the Ten Commandments and the Golden Rule. Although later deleted, their adoption was an effort to impose an ethical code that was both divinely inspired and humanly unenforceable.

Another general rule that speaks to most kinds of misconduct requires officials facing ethical dilemmas to consider how they would feel if their action were publicized on the next morning's front page. Assuming that the action was discovered and published by an aggressive reporter, would your family or friends approve? The station house sergeant in "Hill Street Blues" once told a cop, "Don't worry about department policy. Just ask yourself, 'What would Sarge do in a case like this?' " There are many public servants with the highest ethical standards whom we could name in something like the "Sarge" test.

However, experience demonstrates the value of going beyond those general rules and truisms. In the lawyers' *Code of Professional Responsibility*, there are nine canons. Those are general, aspirational statements, but they are not the basis for lawyer discipline. Rather, the more specific "Disciplinary Rules" are used to measure unethical conduct. The simplicity of the West Point Honor Code is attractive: "A cadet will not lie, cheat, or steal, nor tolerate those who do." That code, however, is enforced in an atmosphere quite different from public life.

It is unfair to discipline or censure someone for acting unethically unless the rules are understandable and relatively specific. While we do not

propose to "disbar" public officials, if we are to hold them truly accountable, the standards of behavior must be as clear as possible. If an official's
ethics are an issue in a political campaign or confirmation hearing, the
"newspaper" test or the "Sarge" test is at best a vague indictment. But
if a specific provision of an ethics code adopted by a government agency
or political party has been violated, the ethics issue will be much clearer.

One point that should not require elaboration is that public servants
ought to obey the law. Yet there are numerous examples of officials elected
despite widespread knowledge of their failure to file income tax returns
or comply with other legal requirements. Sometimes, legislators are reelected while serving prison sentences. Recently, the thirteen-member
city council in Kansas City, Missouri, included one member who went
to prison for income tax violations, six others who paid city taxes late,
and three members who broke the state's open meetings law. A local
reporter wrote, "Notice a trend? It doesn't appear that new laws or ethics
requirements will be a natural top priority here. The city, state and federal
governments already have plenty of laws to govern the conduct of public
officials." Chicago Mayor Richard M. Daley recently surprised officials,
including his own press secretary, whose cars were towed from traditional
but illegal parking spots around City Hall. That was a powerful symbolic
move in a city where it was thought necessary to post "No Tipping"
signs in government offices. If public servants cannot be trusted to obey
the laws that apply to everyone, can they be trusted to obey laws that
apply specifically to them?

A detailed but not exhaustive list of ethical rules for public servants is
a statement of applied ethics—specific statements of desired conduct
based on underlying ethical principles. The underlying principles might
be, for example, "Seek the greatest good for society" or "Honesty is
more important than efficiency." Those principles will vary, and sometimes they conflict. But a proper statement of (applied) ethics for public
officials will have been rigorously tested against those principles. Therefore, before proposing a set of uniform rules concerning the ethical behavior of public servants, we must articulate a philosophy of public service
to use in measuring the utility of specific rules.

The value of hammering out the basic philosophy is illustrated by the
differing ways in which legal ethics and business ethics are taught. All
American law schools require completion of a course in legal ethics. There
are two slightly different statements of legal ethics—the *Code of Professional Responsibility* and the *Model Rules of Professional Conduct*. Most
law school ethics courses are only able to discuss those rules and the
most common violations.

However, because there is no widely accepted statement of business
ethics, an ethics course in an MBA program begins with the philosophical
theory on which (applied) business ethics is based. Proposed ethical rules

for a company or an industry are tested against that theory, rather than studied only as practically applied. The difference is that the business student ought to have a better foundation for evaluating gray areas or new situations for which there is no specific rule. The law student can only reason by analogy from an existing rule and is less able to articulate why a rule is fair or right.

THE HONEST PERSON RULE

> The whole art of government consists in the art of being honest.
> —Thomas Jefferson, "Draft of Instructions to the
> Virginia Delegates in the Continental Congress," August 1774

Skeptics argue that no set of ethics rules is meaningful in any field unless the people involved are basically honest. The notion is that ethics in politics and government are really no different than ethics in personal life. Therefore, people who do not lie, cheat, or steal in business or personal life should have no problem handling ethical questions in government. This view necessarily downplays the importance of rules and focuses more on character. However, many public officials accused of acting unethically are *not* personally dishonest. Even when their unethical conduct also violates a law, it is hard to think of them as criminal. President Nixon's famous "I am not a crook" is a basically correct claim, even if he did break the law.

The Watergate scandal of the mid–1970s is the seminal influence on contemporary political ethics. In the past there were few investigations of officeholders who became much wealthier while in public office. It was accepted that local sheriffs could not maintain their standard of living on a sheriff's meager salary alone. Or, if a governor was an attorney, it was a foregone conclusion that his "former" law firm would prosper greatly during his term. Other examples of changed expectations have occurred in campaign fund-raising practices. The excesses of the 1972 Nixon reelection campaign, which squeezed money from key business leaders and advised them on circumventing disclosure requirements, were not qualitatively different from earlier campaigns.

The experience of the Reagan administration illustrates the difficulty of relying on the basic honesty of officeholders to prevent impropriety. More than a hundred of the honest, well-respected people who entered the highest levels of government encountered the "sleaze factor" and left government under a cloud of suspicion because they acted as if they were still in the private sector, without a specially heightened sensitivity to ethical questions. After the enactment of the 1978 Ethics in Government Act, the rules of conduct for federal officials changed, and scrutiny of their conduct became intensive. While the Reagan appointees should have known the new rules, it is hard to change habits and long-standing political customs. They were not basically dishonest people. Without excusing their conduct, the ethical violations are not explained by character defects that should have been detected.

BALANCING TWO OPPOSING PRINCIPLES

As mentioned earlier, codes of medical or legal ethics are statements of applied ethics—the application of underlying ethical principles and philosophies to a specific profession. At the risk of oversimplifying the work of philosophers, public service ethics are formed by the clash of two basic viewpoints: utilitarian versus deontological. The utilitarian believes that the end sought (e.g., efficiency, economy) justifies the means to that end. The deontologist believes that certain absolute principles (e.g., honesty) should be obeyed, regardless of the consequences. In real life, none of us is exclusively utilitarian or deontological. Our personal values reflect a mix of those viewpoints, depending on the issue. Sometimes we act solely as a matter of principle (deontological) and sometimes we act practically (utilitarian). Frequently, our ethical choices are explained by a compromise between the two.

No statement of public service ethics will be entirely in one camp or the other. Like our personal ethical life, the accepted position on certain issues will seem utilitarian, while on others the middle ground is based on firm principles. Successful public servants cannot wholly rely on either. They face problems in the gray areas in between. For example, while we generally disfavor lying by public officials, a false leak to the press to provide cover for a sensitive military or diplomatic mission is not viewed by most people as wrong. However, perjury before a congressional committee on the same matter would be inexcusable. The subtle differences between the contexts of the lie sometimes elude officials—to their great surprise. The lie or deception inherent in an undercover law enforcement operation is acceptable unless it goes so far as to become entrapment, snaring people who otherwise would not commit the crime.

The term for politics, the "art of the possible,"[4] recognizes the numerous compromises and manipulations necessary for an effective political system. Two opposing viewpoints each think of themselves as taking the truly ethical position. But in order to pass a law or negotiate a treaty, each side must be willing to settle for less than its ideal. Otherwise, there is deadlock. Claes G. Ryn wrote, "It can even be said that it is a moral duty for the politician to adjust his means to the circumstances, that is, to adopt a pragmatic approach, for this is the only way in which some progress towards the ethical goal can be made."[5] West Virginia Supreme Court Justice Richard Neely believes there is a Laffer Curve in political ethics.[6] At one end, an absolutely ethical government would be frozen in action, while an absolutely corrupt government would grind to a halt because all resources and taxes would be stolen. Only somewhere in the middle is there the right balance of ethics versus self-interest and honesty versus service to constituents and contributors. Only somewhere in the middle does government work efficiently.

Regardless of which underlying ethical theory makes most sense to you, both deontology and utilitarianism share the common goal that the greater good be produced. In public service ethics, we are not concerned about the greatest good for public servants, although we do need to attract the most talented and honest people to government. Rather, we want to create the greatest good for society, including economy, efficiency, optimum public safety and other services, and "good feelings"—pride, patriotism, national self-worth. We know, for example, that unethical behavior is not cost efficient. Higher taxes and/or lower levels of services result if fair, competitive bidding practices are ignored. Political hacks run agencies less efficiently than capable, but less-politicized bureaucrats. (At the same time, elected officials may be much better at providing constituent services than unresponsive bureaucrats.) Corruptly ignored building codes or safety violations may cost money and lives.

An atmosphere of corruption makes it more difficult to attract good people to serve in government. Massachusetts Governor William F. Weld wrote,

A perception that the system is corrupt or rigged will, by a political Gresham's law, eventually drive the good players out of the game. I saw that happen in Massachusetts.... Many reputable contractors, architects, and engineers simply refused to bid on government contracts. Beyond a certain point, if we acquiesce in the notion that politics and public life are a 'dirty business,' we are going to dissuade honest and able citizens from seeking public office in the first place.[7]

THE ROLE OF THE EGO

A major theme in any study of ethics is the importance of self-interest. In *The Wealth of Nations* Adam Smith argued that the lightly regulated pursuit of self-interest by businessmen would, over time, generate the greatest economic good. Today, Milton Friedman minimizes the social responsibility of business when he argues that the only role of business is to make profits. The self-interest of public servants is equally important, but different. The actions of an officeholder to increase his or her net worth while in office is exactly the kind of self-interest that leads to the most obvious ethical problems. However, the self-interest of desiring a good reputation or the honor of a high position ought to cause the public servant to be both effective and scrupulous. The satisfaction from being in public life should motivate the public servant in the same way that economic self-interest drives the businessperson.

Both the public official and the businessperson have mixed motives. The public official does have financial demands and is concerned about job security (except for federal judges), pay raises, and the possibility of returning to the private sector. And the businessperson wants a reputation as a community leader and sponsor of charitable works. However, the dominant goal of their everyday work ought to be dramatically different.

Joel Fleishman of Duke University summarized the proper commitments of a public official:

First, there is a deep personal commitment to principles grounded in the public interest.

Second, there is commitment to the public interest as a whole—the greater good of the greatest number over the long run rather than to particular interests over the short run.

Third, there is commitment to protection of deserving minority interests when threatened by majorities and to the advancement of the welfare of those *undeservedly* less well off.

Fourth, there is consistency of dedication over time.

Fifth, there is honesty with the public and with one's fellow officials.

Sixth, there is independence of judgment, even, perhaps especially, when the personal political risk is high, coupled with a zeal to persuade one's constituents of the wisdom of one's point of view. The greatest public leaders of all time are those who brought the public to accept *their* point of view, who did not reflect public opinion, but molded it.

Finally, there is humility, which comes very hard to anyone who exercises power over others, whether in the public or the private sector, in part because it is, at least superficially, the antithesis of ego, which is what drives self-interest. And yet, if one pursues what one perceives to be the public interest long enough, one can gradually use it as a lever to gain control over one's ego.[8]

In legal ethics, there is always a conflict of interest between the lawyer and client over the matter of the fee. The only way to completely avoid that conflict would be for lawyers to renounce wealth. Public servants may be as unable as lawyers to renounce wealth, but they must be primarily motivated by satisfactions from their work rather than a desire to become wealthy.

AN ETHICAL PREMISE

Public officials are obligated to render honest judgment, to work hard and efficiently, and to maximize the benefits of government to all citizens.

This premise is the basis for all the remaining discussion about proper ethical standards for public officials. Each specific rule ought to be consistent with it. *Public officials* are defined as government employees, whether career or appointed, and elected officials at every level of government.

BASIC PRINCIPLES

Based on that premise, there are certain self-evident rules of conduct for all public servants that are not addressed at length in the following chapters.

1. Public officials must not lie, cheat, or steal in any official capacity. They must obey the law. Public officials must always tell the truth to the public, other governmental bodies, and the press, except in extremely limited circumstances, such as war or national emergency, when a temporary deception serves a paramount governmental purpose.

2. Public officials must avoid all conflicts of interest created by business, friendship, or family relationships and must always be careful to avoid even the appearance of impropriety.

3. Public officials owe a fiduciary duty to taxpayers and all citizens to ensure that public funds are used efficiently. Officials and all public employees whom they supervise should be as productive as possible.

4. Public officials must not allow zeal for their duties, including such duties as tax collection or law enforcement, to cause them to violate citizens' legal rights. Public servants should not be rude or unresponsive when dealing with the public.

5. Public officials should cooperate with other officials and agencies to maximize the public good, rather than acting out of cronyism or advancing the interests of politicians or a political machine.

6. Public officials should perform their duties based solely on the public good, rather than what is in their best political interests. They should not pressure public employees to assist in the official's political career or reelection efforts.

NOTES

1. C. G. Ryn DEMOCRACY AND THE ETHICAL LIFE: A PHILOSOPHY OF POLITICS AND COMMUNITY 9 (2d ed. 1990).

2. *Ethics Embarrassment May Kick Congress into Action*, Bus. Wk., Feb. 20, 1989, at 43.

3. REPORT OF THE PRESIDENT'S COMMISSION ON FEDERAL ETHICS LAW REFORM, Mar. 1989, at 1.

4. Prince Otto Von Bismark, conversation with Meyer Von Waldeck (Aug. 11, 1867; "*Die Politick ist die Lehre von Moglichen*," reprinted in D. Baker, POLITICAL QUOTATIONS (1990).

5. Ryn, *supra* note 1, at 22.

6. Letter from Justice Richard Neely to Richard Wentworth, April 1, 1991.

7. Weld, *Public Corruption Is Costing Us Too Much*, Wash. Post May 2–8, 1988, at 22 (nat'l wkly. ed.).

8. J. L. Fleishman, *Keynote Address: The Pursuit of Self-Interest for the Public Good: An Ethical Paradox of Representative Democracy*.

2

Financing Election Campaigns

Most misconduct by elected officials can be traced, directly or indirectly, to campaign financing. As the late California Democrat Jesse Unruh said, "Money is the mother's milk of politics." The question is this: Can we and should we wean the candidates from their contributors? The pressure does not end with the election. The IOUs of major donors come back to haunt the elected official. In addition, there will be compromises and neglect of duty caused by the need to pay off campaign debts or to start raising money early for the next campaign. U.S. senators must raise an average of $12,500 each week for six years in order to prepare for the next election.[1]

Relatively few campaign contributions are from private citizens who merely wish to support a politician who represents their political views or whom they like personally. The vast majority are from special interests—businesses, unions, and wealthy individuals who want influence and access. For example, in New York, more than 90 percent of the comptroller's campaign funds in a three-year period came from industries that did business with his office. Over a five-year period, more than 90 percent of the engineers who received contracts from the State Department of Transportation and the Thruway Authority made contributions to the State Democratic Party or Governor Cuomo's campaign committee. By contrast, it is news when candidates running for city council refuse to accept campaign contributions from developers.

One poll showed that public esteem for members of Congress fell from 61 percent to 51 percent between April 1989 and February 1990, with about one-third of the voters stating the belief that their representatives were "caught up and corrupted by the system of money and politics."[2] Challengers in political races are beginning to make campaign finance an issue by calling for voluntary limits on spending or contributions. Because those limits benefit the challenger more than the incumbent, they are rarely accepted.

The case of the Keating Five illustrates the problem. Five senators took a total of $1.3 million in direct and indirect contributions from a savings and loan operator who then requested their assistance in stalling government interference with the way he conducted business. The chairman of the Senate Ethics Committee, Senator Howell Heflin, opened the Keating Five hearings by saying, "Many of our fellow citizens apparently believe that your services were bought by Charles Keating; that you were bribed, that you sold your office, that you traded your honor and your good names for contributions and other benefits."[3] Fred Wertheimer, president of Common Cause, said, "To really understand what happened here, citizens have to ask themselves what would happen if they tried to get five senators to intervene for them in a government enforcement proceeding. The answer is, it would never happen."[4]

However, their willingness to accept S&L money was not isolated. During the 1980s, S&L interests contributed more than $11 million to congressional candidates. The senator who received the most money in direct contributions, now California Governor Pete Wilson, collected $243,334 from S&L-related individuals and entities during that time.

During the fall of 1990, so many fund-raisers were being held simultaneously in certain Washington restaurants that candidates began holding "no-show" fund-raisers, allowing contributors to mail in checks without having to face more hors d'oeuvres. Pete Wilson and Diane Feinstein spent up to 90 percent of their time raising money during the last few weeks of the 1990 California gubernatorial campaign.

The root of the problem is the cost of unregulated campaigning. In 1976, the cost of an average winning senatorial campaign was $610,000. In 1988, it was $3,600,000. One factor in Governor Pete Wilson's appointment of someone to his Senate seat was the expense of the confirmation election in 1992 and another election in 1994, when Wilson's term would otherwise have ended. The cost of those two back-to-back elections could easily exceed $20 million.[5] Without an effective ceiling on the amount that can be spent on campaigns, politicians will continue to try to outspend each other. By early 1991, several California congressmen jockeying to succeed Senator Alan Cranston in 1992 had raised nearly $2 million each.

The only way to put an effective cap on campaign expenditures is a system of public financing for campaigns, an idea discussed later in this chapter. Another approach, limiting the amount that can be contributed, is also problematical. In 1988, California voters approved a measure to limit contributions to $1,000 from individuals and $5,000 from political action committees (PACs) for each fiscal year. Politicians said that the law simply forced them to look for more small donations, rather than relying on a relatively few fat cats. However, in the last few weeks before the 1990 elections, a federal judge declared the law unconstitutional because it gave incumbents an unfair advantage. They could solicit contributions each year, planning for the next race, while challengers could not plan that far in advance.[6] Furthermore, incumbents are more likely to collect money during nonelection years, even in the unlikely event that a challenger announces his or her candidacy years in advance of the election.

The need to raise large amounts of money has given birth to ingenious schemes. In 1990, the National Republican Senatorial Committee sent $25 checks to one million prospective contributors. On the back of the check was fine print authorizing the committee, if the check was endorsed, to deduct $12.50 per month from the recipients' checking accounts. Several state attorney generals investigated the device to determine whether it was deceptive, although a spokesperson for the committee said that the accompanying letter clearly explained the automatic withdrawal arrangement.

MONEY TALKS

> I think I can say, and say with pride, that we have some legislatures that bring higher prices than any in the world.
> —Mark Twain, *Sketches, New and Old* (1875)

Representative Andy Jacobs said, "Campaign contributions are not terribly different from a bribe. The only reason it is not bribery is because Congress defines what bribery is."[7] Although no candid politician denies the link between contributions and influence, the elaborate etiquette is breached if a contributor ever explicitly demands a favor because of a contribution. If that occurs, the legislator is overcome with righteous indignation and may throw the contributor out of the office. But so long as the etiquette is observed, it is business as usual.

For example, Ohio Senator Howard Metzenbaum attended a 1987 cocktail party/fund-raiser at which he spoke for ten minutes and shook hands. He collected $80,000 in campaign contributions from attendees—lawyers and labor leaders interested in a specialized workers' compensation law for the railroad industry, which Senator Metzenbaum vigorously defends.[8] No one could claim that Senator Metzenbaum was bribed by special interests; his legislative conduct on that issue has been consistent over many years. He merely collected money from people who supported his view on that particular issue.

Senator Robert Kasten of Wisconsin consistently opposes Senator Metzenbaum on aspects of the railroad employees' workers' compensation law. Not coincidentally, he receives PAC contributions from the railroad industry.[9] Neither of these respected senators is acting unethically in this example, but it illustrates the problem with appearances. Those donations contribute to an appearance that legitimate legislative and political views are influenced by the source of campaign contributions.

Congressman Robert Dornan, known for his brilliant use of direct mail to raise millions in small contributions, says that his success at raising money by direct mail relieves him of having to ask for large contributions. He said, "You're asking someone to give you a big chunk of change . . . and hope that they're not going to call you . . . and yell at you: 'Gee, I helped you and now you're going the opposite way.' "[10]

YOUR BEST BUY SINCE 1972

The key event in the development of campaign financing reform was the 1972 Republican presidential fund-raising effort. Former House Speaker Tip O'Neill, no political innocent, described the unsubtle linkage between a businessman's failure to give at a satisfactory level and problems with governmental contracts or the IRS:

The conclusion was inescapable: what we had was an old-fashioned shakedown. I thought I had seen it all, but never in my life had I seen outright blackmail. . . . If this was how these guys played the game when they had already won, what would they try if they ever found themselves in a really tough fight?[11]

In 1974, Congress established the Federal Election Commission (FEC) to regulate the financing of all federal election campaigns. Between 1974 and 1978, twenty-seven states created agencies to regulate campaign financing or ethics in government. The major features of these reforms were (1) disclosure of the source and amount of contributions, (2) disclosures about PACs, which were created to make contributions that corporations could not make directly to candidates, and (3) limitations on the amount that individuals could give directly to campaigns.

These reforms, like all similar efforts, vary widely among states and have numerous loopholes. One obvious deficiency of any campaign financing reform is that it cannot constitutionally restrict a candidate's own spending. A wealthy candidate may outspend opponents who rely entirely on contributions. In Nashville, Tennessee, a respected but little-known businessman sold his business interests for $27 million and then poured several million dollars of his own money into a series of election campaigns and runoffs for different offices. He made a virtue of the fact that he would not be obligated to donors. He bought name recognition far greater than most new candidates ever receive. In 1989 one of the New York City mayoral candidates who opted out of public financing was the cosmetics heir Ronald S. Lauder, who spent more than $10 million of his own money in his losing effort. Senator John D. Rockefeller IV spent $10 million of his own money on his 1984 election.

Rich politicians have an ability to publicize themselves that is not available to other, equally well-qualified people. Their money can win name recognition that was not earned by past political efforts or public service. We cannot legally restrict such outlandish spending, but we can vote against excess.

The utopian solution to campaign financing excesses would require a constitutional amendment to change the current interpretation of the First Amendment right of free speech in the form of campaign contributions. Combined with a broad-based, equitable method of public campaign financing, that would permit a return to a purer form of democracy in which ideas and character matter more than media and marketshare.

The citizens' group Common Cause distributed flyers and postcards urging members of Congress to "Take the Keating Test," referring to the Keating Five. It asked the members to answer Yes or No to the following questions:

Do You Agree that "soft money" contributions must be banned to prevent "fat cat" contributors, like S&L owner Charles Keating, corporations and labor unions, from making contributions of $100,000 or more to support presidential and congressional candidates?

Do You Agree that political action committee (PAC) contributions to congressional candidates must be dramatically reduced to prevent special interests, like the S&L industry, from contributing huge amounts of influence money to Members of Congress?

Do You Agree that limits on skyrocketing campaign spending must be established to stop the never-ending chase for campaign contributions that sends Members of Congress running to private interests like Charles Keating and the PACs for political money?

Do You Agree that alternative campaign funds must be provided to ensure that "clean" campaign resources, such as public matching funds and low-cost mailings, are available so Members of Congress aren't dependent on money from influence seekers?[12]

Common Cause and the overwhelming majority of Americans would consider the correct answer to those questions to be *Yes*.

THE PACMAN COMETH

A gradual but incredible change has occurred in the U.S. House of Representatives. Members who nominally must run for reelection every two years have acquired tenure, the near-certainty of reelection. In 1988, 99 percent of incumbents seeking reelection won. There was more turnover on the Soviet Communist Party's Central Committee.[13] Furthermore, 82 percent of the races were landslides. (Four of the six members who lost were involved in misconduct or scandal.) A similar change has occurred in state legislatures. For example, also in 1988, 98 percent of the incumbents who ran for reelection to the Missouri General Assembly won.

With the benefits of free staff and franking privileges incumbents have always enjoyed advantages over challengers. The technology of elections, including polling and sophisticated direct mail, also favors the candidate with the most money to spend. Now, an incumbent is almost always the candidate with the most money. An incumbent with a huge war chest on hand will discourage the best opponents, who see the race as futile. The consensus explanation for this change is the structure of campaign financing. And the principal feature of that structure is the PAC.

The first PACs were formed by labor unions after 1943, when it became illegal for unions to contribute directly to congressional candidates. The dramatic rise of business PACs followed the imposition of strict $1,000 limits on campaign contributions in federal elections made directly to candidates by individuals and the ban on direct corporate contributions. In a 1990 decision, the Supreme Court upheld a state's prohibition on direct corporate contributions in *Austin v. Michigan Chamber of Commerce*.[14] The Court held that although the law burdened the corporation's First Amendment right of political expression, the burden was justified by the interest in preventing corruption and the appearance of corruption in campaign financing.

Currently, federal law permits industries, particular companies, unions, and citizens to donate up to $5,000 dollars each to an unlimited number of PACs who then make the contributions. In federal campaigns, a PAC may contribute up to $10,000 per candidate. There are almost 5,000 PACs. During 1989–90, the largest corporate PAC was AT&T, which raised $2.8 million. The largest trade association PAC, the American Medical Association, raised $5.7 million. One union PAC collects ten cents per month from each union member. AutoPAC, representing the import automobile business, encourages car dealers to donate $1 for each car sold.[15]

In California, the twenty-five largest PACs donated almost $9 million to state campaigns in the months leading up to the 1990 elections. Even in a small state like Tennessee, one-fourth of the money raised in recent state campaigns came from PACs. PACs are less influential in states that have not banned direct corporate contributions to state campaigns.

PACs favor incumbents. In the 1988 election, House incumbents received about *seventeen times* as much PAC money as did challengers. More than $15 million in PAC money went to House members who were unopposed. In the 1990 elections, for example, 70 percent of House Speaker Thomas Foley's campaign funds came from PACs, compared to 5 percent for his opponent. PACs are unwilling to give significant sums to challengers who may not win and thereby offend the incumbent, who has power over them. If an incumbent loses, PACs try to gain favor by paying off the challenger's campaign debt. Better late than never. PACs also favor Democrats generally, because most incumbents are Democrats. In 1988, congressional Democrats received $75 million while congressional Republicans received only $45 million.[16] Not surprisingly, Republicans are interested in PAC reform.

The leading proposal for PAC reform is that PACs should be allowed to contribute only to political parties. The parties will then distribute money to candidates. That does not remove all the ethical problems. For example, it does not prevent the laundering of campaign money that goes on now. Currently, federal law permits each PAC to give up to $15,000 to a political party. A PAC will do so when a direct contribution to a candidate would harm the candidate. For example, if an incumbent from the Northeast, which is generally hostile to oil interests, took money from oil and gas PACs, an opponent could benefit from the resulting publicity. But if the PAC contributes the maximum to the party, the party can pass that money through to the candidate without the taint. Florida's new campaign finance law partially solves that problem by limiting a party's contribution to a candidate to $50,000 in a single campaign.

It may be more ethical for a PAC to distribute money to candidates who most closely share the PAC's political view, whether challenger or incumbent. Or it may be unethical for PACs to contribute to officials running unopposed. PACs will distribute money in ways that seem to advance their interests. However, we are primarily concerned with the ethics of the candidates and potential candidates. Tammany Hall politician George Washington Plunkitt said, "The day may come when we'll reject the money of the rich as tainted, but it hadn't come when I left Tammany Hall at 11:25 A.M. today."[17] A longtime contemporary politician, the late Congressman Richard Bolling, framed the issue concretely: "If you had two phone calls at once, and your secretary said one was a constituent and the other a PAC that gave you $10,000 last election, which phone would you pick up?"[18] A politician's willingness to take money from PACs is one of the clearest indicators of his or her sense of ethics.

While every PAC is interested in legislation on which all legislators may vote, the impropriety is greater when the PAC represents a specific company or industry that the legislator directly oversees. For example, during the investigation of Pentagon contracting practices, it was learned that members of the four congressional committees supervising military procurement received enormous campaign contributions, as well as "speaking fees," from defense industry PACs.[19] Almost one-half of all the defense contractor PAC money went to members on those committees.

The fifty-two members of the House Banking Committee received $3,254,040 from PACs representing banking, insurance, and real estate interests during 1989–90. The head of the American Banker's Association PAC said that PAC contributions are designed to provide access to legislators: "There's no way you can buy somebody's vote for ten thousand bucks. What we try to do is get our foot in the door."[20]

Another abuse of PAC money occurs when candidates with surplus campaign funds contribute to their own PAC, which then contributes to the campaign of another candidate, thereby ensuring political friendship and loyalty. More than seventy members of Congress have their own PACs, known as "leadership" PACs. Contributing PACs can give to the candidate's campaign, the candidate's PAC, or both. Congressional leadership positions may go to those whose PACs contributed to the most legislators. Therefore, contributions to a candidate's PAC not only buy influence and access with the legislator, but may also help the friendly legislator rise to positions of greater power, where the influence and access will be even more valuable.

PUBLIC FINANCING

The best way to minimize the corrupting influence of campaign contributions is a system of public financing of elections. In New York City, a candidate can qualify for funds to match small private contributions up to $500 in exchange for limitations on both contributions and expenditures. In 1989 citywide races, all but two candidates participated, but only about half of City Council members enrolled. A mayoral candidate who accepted public funds was limited to spending $3 million in the primary, $1.5 million in a primary runoff, and another $3 million in the general election. In 1991, Florida linked acceptance of public financing to a voluntary cap of $5 million for gubernatorial races and $2 million for other elected members of the Governor's Cabinet.

No system of public financing or restrictions on private giving to candidates is likely to resolve all ethical questions. However, increased scrutiny of campaign finances leads to a generally heightened sense of public service ethics. In some states, the early effort to regulate the disclosure of political giving was the basis for broader governmental ethics laws.

Twenty-two states, as well as the federal government, have various public finance mechanisms for election campaigns. Like the federal system, most are funded by a checkoff provision on state income tax forms.

In exchange for public funds, the candidates forego other kinds of fund raising and agree to certain limits on campaign receipts and expenditures. Three states—Minnesota, Wisconsin, and Hawaii—fund campaigns for virtually every state office, including local and municipal offices. Thirteen states fund political parties, and six states fund all or some of the statewide races.

Public financing does not address the disparity caused by wealthy candidates, because the Supreme Court held in a 1976 case, *Buckley v. Valeo*,[21] that candidates' personal spending can be limited only if they accept public financing. However, Florida's new public campaign finance laws make it unlikely that even a wealthy candidate would refuse the public money and accompanying spending limits. If one candidate opts out, the candidate who participated in public financing is given funds equal to the amount by which his or her opponent exceeded the limit.

In states with broad-based public financing of campaigns, candidate participation is high. In Minnesota, the acceptance rates have been as high as 83.2 percent for Republicans and 96.9 percent for Democrats. However, in a state like Iowa, which directs public funds to political parties, the parties decide which candidates in which races will receive support. That may leave individual candidates in the position of trying to raise campaign funds from influence buyers and PACs. Also, any formula for distributing public money to political parties will impede the development or campaigning of third party or independent candidates.

Another model of state public finance is New Jersey, which comprehensively funds only campaigns for governor. Public funding is the dominant source of money for New Jersey gubernatorial primaries, as well as for the general election. If a state attempts comprehensive funding of campaigns for numerous positions, as does Hawaii, there will not be a significant amount of money available for all races.

The deadlock over expanded federal financing of congressional campaigns is illustrated by the difference between two recent reform bills introduced in the Senate. The Democratic bill would pay 70 percent of the expenses of the general election, but none in the primaries, and limit total expenditures in the general election to a scale ranging from $1.9 million in small states to more than $10 million in California, the largest state. It also proposes banning PAC contributions to individual candidates but permitting them to contribute to political parties. The Republican proposal would ban union and corporate PACs completely and permit ideological, issue-oriented PACs to contribute only $2,000 per candidate. However, the Republican bill does not limit the total amounts that candidates can raise from individuals or spend on elections. The voting on recent Senate efforts at reform followed party lines, and President Bush has indicated he would veto any bill that includes public subsidies of campaigns.

Public financing of campaigns would relieve many of the pressures on candidates that result in improper influence by wealthy and powerful groups, as well as the appearance of impropriety. However, only an effective and well-funded plan such as Minnesota's will make most candidates accept the public financing alternative. Candidates accept it only when they are convinced that their opponents can obtain no advantage by opting out of the public financing plan. More states should enact public financing laws, and more taxpayers should use the checkoff provision to direct tax money toward public campaign financing. It is hypocritical to complain about crooked or insensitive politicians scrounging for money from interest groups but not to check off tax dollars to public financing of political campaigns.

Any effort at comprehensive campaign reform must also address "soft" money—contributions that further a candidate's chances but are not made directly to the candidate's campaign. The leading source of soft money is political parties that direct funds to particular candidates. For example, in Poughkeepsie, New York, a development company named Pyramid wanted to influence a 1985 Town Board election in order to get property rezoned. There was a limit of $1,000 on contributions to Town Board candidates. So, nineteen Pyramid partners and their relatives directed more than $300,000 in contributions to two political party committees and a PAC with the understanding that the money would be passed along to the pro-Pyramid candidates. The anti-Pyramid candidates were outspent fifteen to one, but Pyramid remained invisible to the voters.[22] At least those contributions and expenditures must be disclosed and can be tracked. Eventually.

That is not true of another source of soft money, tax-exempt voter registration charities. One of the Keating Five, Senator Cranston, raised millions of dollars for those charities in donations as large as $400,000. Charles Keating donated $850,000 to three voter registration groups with which Senator Cranston was involved. In a 1986 memo to donors, the senator wrote, "Remember, in addition to being tax deductible, these contributions may be unlimited in amount and need not be publicly reported."[23] During the 1988 elections, both parties solicited $100,000 gifts to those activities.

The FEC has not strictly regulated the use of contributions for voter registration drives benefiting both state and presidential candidates. The FEC has been described as a toothless watchdog. Four votes are required before the FEC can act, but the six-member commission has three members from each party.

A final loophole is direct spending by PACs that are technically independent of particular candidates although they frequently share consultants and campaign advisers with the candidates whom they help. Independent spending by a PAC may be decisive, especially in the last few days of a campaign, by paying for a media blitz that attacks the candidate opposed to its interests. In the 1988 elections, Florida Senator Connie Mack beat his opponent by just 33,000 votes. In the week before the election, AutoPAC, the import automobile industry PAC, spent $326,000 on hard-hitting television ads in support of Mack.

THE REMEDY OF DISCLOSURE

If contributions must be disclosed at some point, the public can make judgments about candidates based on the source and amount of campaign contributions and can identify later actions by the official involving campaign donors. Georgia's Ethics in Government Act begins,

It is declared to be the policy of this state, in furtherance of its responsibility to protect the integrity of the democratic process and to ensure fair elections . . . to institute and establish a requirement of public disclosure of campaign contributions and expenditures relative to the seeking of such offices, to the recall of public officers holding elective office, and to the influencing of voter approval or rejection of a proposed constitutional amendment, a state-wide referendum, or a proposed question which is to appear on the ballot in any county or municipal election.[24]

The Georgia law is more rigorous than the average state disclosure law. It excludes contributions or expenditures of $100 or less, both to minimize the paperwork and because there is less danger of impropriety arising from small contributions. Although contributions raise the most concern, the reporting of campaign expenditures is also important because both the amounts and the patterns of spending tell us about the candidates' priorities and whether they are rewarding friends. Or themselves. One former congressman used campaign funds to buy sophisticated computers and direct mail equipment for a business he owned. Other congressmen have used campaign cash to buy $30,000 cars and $12,500 worth of Broadway show tickets, while Representative Edward R. Roybal used $100,000 of campaign donations to endow a chair in his name at UCLA. A *Los Angeles Times* study showed that 65 percent of campaign spending by incumbent congressmen had little or nothing to do with directly winning the support of voters.[25]

However, the Georgia law has an easily abused feature common to most disclosure laws. The last report before the election must be filed fifteen days before the election. The next report must be filed on or before December 31 of the election year. Large special interest contributors can wait until the fourteenth day to make their contributions, which will not be reported until weeks or months later. Nor does this tactic interfere with early heavy spending by a candidate who may be able to borrow money with the assurance that late contributions will pay off loans.

Candidates should disclose more information and disclose it more often than most disclosure laws require. If that is a tactical disadvantage, it is balanced by the advantage of claiming that the candidate's high sense of ethics is demonstrated by the willingness to do more than the law requires. The "clean" candidate can argue that the opponent who only complies with the minimum disclosure required by law may have something to hide.

Disclosure requirements ought to be tightened and the loopholes minimized. Candidates should welcome disclosure, unlike Congressman Dan Rostenkowski, who has his disclosure forms typed in a difficult-to-read Old English script. With the modern computer equipment that most campaigns use, there should be continuous, up-to-the-minute reporting.

Every level of government needs a comprehensive law about campaign disclosure that provides for effective enforcement. However, no such law can serve as the only statement about the ethics of the candidate, who is either a current or prospective public official. While the public attention that disclosure of contributions and expenditures invites is valuable, it does not address the more fundamental ethical issues: What do candidates promise, explicitly or implicitly, to donors? Should candidates spend most of their time raising money? Should they know who their contributors are?

IN THE DARK

Trial judges in many states are elected and are governed by the general campaign funds reporting law, which requires the candidates to certify that the attached list of donors and amounts is correct. One judicial candidate in Tennessee, Matt Sweeney, saw a conflict between his duty under that law to certify that the contributions list was accurate and a principle of judicial ethics that a judicial candidate should not know who contributed to the campaign. Therefore, he refused to comply with the law. No action was taken against him because the authorities recognized the ethical dilemma. Judge Sweeney relied on his campaign treasurer's certification that the list of contributions was accurate.

Other candidates should take the same position. By declaring that the campaign treasurer was in charge of raising and reporting contributions, the candidate would make a strong statement about ethics and minimize the chance that contributors would expect or receive special treatment later. Such a candidate would present an unusually clear choice against an opponent who receives special interest money in the normal way.

An incidental, but significant, benefit of a hands-off approach to fund raising is that the candidate would have the time to actually campaign with the people or to think about the issues. There is no doubt that the candidates would prefer to avoid the fund-raising process. Senator Hubert Humphrey, the Happy Warrior, called it "the most disgusting, demeaning, disenchanting, debilitating experience of a politician's life. It's stinky, it's lousy. I just can't tell you how much I hate it."[26]

The hands-off approach is the ideal model. Few candidates would risk offending donors by failing to ask for money themselves or to promptly return donors' phone calls. Few candidates would send a campaign treasurer or other fund raiser to the cocktail parties and "rubber chicken dinners" where campaign funds are collected. Most candidates fear that their opponents would still be willing to engage in the mating dance between candidate and contributors—the courtship rituals that convince contributors that the candidate knows who they are, appreciates them, and will repay the donation with influence and access. The brave candidates who stake a claim to a higher ethical standard and distance themselves from campaign financing will be derided as being unable to raise money even if they wanted to.

Candidates should at least make it perfectly clear that the contributions are appreciated and the donor's point of view will always be considered but that donations do not buy favors. However, donors may take such a declaration lightly unless they know of examples when the public official backed it up.

Another firm position to take is to refuse all large campaign contributions from any source. Lawton Chiles was elected Florida's governor after refusing to accept contributions of over $100 while running against the corrupting influence of money in politics. He said, "Do I want to destroy the system? I do, with every fiber and bone in my body. Help us make this an election, not an auction."[27] (In his first Senate campaign in 1970, he refused to accept contributions over $10. Inflation!) As Governor, Chiles led the Florida Legislature to pass the toughest limits on contributions to statewide political races, including a $500 contribution limit to any candidate.

A politician who stakes out a reform position on campaign finance should be consistent. A candidate for the powerful California post of Insurance Commissioner, John Garamendi, refused donations from insurance company employees but accepted numerous $500–$1,000 checks from the spouses of insurance company employees. He said that he assumed that the wives were acting on their own behalf.[28] Garamendi won and is currently viewed as a tough regulator, but the appearance of impropriety lingers on.

The ultimate objection to a strong, consistent position that minimizes the influence of campaign contributions is: "If I don't play the game—take the money from PACs and special interests and repay them for their investment in me—I won't be in office and able to do good in other ways. Opponents who will play the game will beat me and they will do less good overall." The answer to that objection will never satisfy the cynic, but it goes like this: The American voters get the kind of government they deserve. If they vote against ethical but underfinanced candidates, they will get lousy government. Eventually, they will come to their senses, voting for ethical candidates and supporting campaign reform that minimizes abuse.

DEBT AND SURPLUS

The ethical dilemma inherent in having candidates raise campaign funds is even greater when the elected official is raising money to pay off campaign debts. Campaign vendors and suppliers must be paid, but post-election fund-raising is an ethical quagmire. The contributors are no longer betting that they may have influence and access. The candidate's victory guarantees it. And it is natural to treat those donors who bail you out of campaign debt even more favorably than preelection contributors. The ethical candidate must carefully avoid campaign debt, rather than gambling on victory with borrowed money or credit, confident that a victor's debt is easily paid. The ethical candidate is once again at a tactical disadvantage, but that is not a persuasive reason to act otherwise.

If there is inadvertent campaign debt, campaign treasurers or other supporters should take the lead in raising money and minimize the public official's role. That may be easier after the election, when a donor is more comfortable dealing with an aide rather than directly with the official. However, the fund-raising surrogates must be equally careful not to promise favors, explicitly or implicitly, in return for contributions.

The happier case, a campaign surplus, is also troubling if its use is unrestricted. Following the 1988 elections, congressional incumbents had $63 million in surplus funds, compared to the $39 million raised and spent by their opponents. Any campaign contributions received when the election is no longer in doubt might as well be made to the candidate's own bank account. Allowing the surplus to be used for the official's personal expenses or as an ongoing political slush fund to support allies is merely an indirect bribe. In addition to the use of candidate-controlled "leadership" PACs to curry favor with other candidates, surplus campaign funds can be directed to once and future colleagues or other politicians.

The use of excess funds to increase the incumbent's power is troubling. Rarely do candidates give the surplus to their political party for distribution to other party candidates. Their claim to influence over or loyalty from the other candidates would be too diluted.

Three California congressmen—Henry Waxman, Howard Berman, and Mel Levine—make joint decisions about donations to other congressional races, as well as state legislative, gubernatorial, and local elections. In the 1990 election cycle, the three congressmen distributed more than $200,000 to other candidates. (During 1987–88, they made 256 contributions totaling more than $450,000.) Congressman Waxman also gave an additional $85,000 through his own PAC. Waxman said,

It clearly builds relationships with colleagues to help them in their elections just as it builds relationships with colleagues to help them with their legislative activities. And those relationships are important because ultimately, to do anything around here, you have to have coalitions and support.[29]

While donating heavily to other candidates with the money donated to them, the congressmen spend little of their campaign funds on their own campaigns. For Berman, the percentage spent on his own campaign was 17 percent; for Waxman, it was 19 percent; and for Levine, it was 35 percent.

The U.S. Senate's rules allow excess campaign funds to be used to supplement the government pay of staffers, the same staffers who are also raising money and performing other political chores for the senator. Senator Sam Nunn's chief of staff received more than $32,000 in consulting fees and expenses from campaign monies during the years leading up to the 1990 elections.

The Georgia campaign financing law permits typical uses of surplus campaign funds. They can be:

1. contributed to any charitable organization;
2. transferred to any national, state, or local committee of any political party or to any candidate;
3. repaid on a pro rata basis to contributors;
4. held for use in any future campaigns for any elective office;
5. applied to campaign debt from prior campaigns;
6. converted to *personal* use if (a) all contributors are notified in writing of the intention to convert funds to personal use and (b) any contributors objecting to the conversion of funds to the candidate's personal use are refunded a pro rata portion of their contribution; or
7. directed in a candidate's will to be spent in any of these ways but, in the absence of such direction in a deceased candidate's will, directed to the treasury of the candidate's political party.[30]

Ethically, the third choice is the best. If contributions were not spent for the purpose for which they were given, the candidate's election campaign, they should be returned. There is little reason to believe that donors would have contributed if they knew that the money would not be used for the candidate's election. The first choice, a gift to charity, sounds wholesome enough, but it may not be a charity to which the campaign donor would have given directly. Furthermore, the gift entitles the official to a charitable deduction against taxable income, an additional benefit to them.

The sixth choice, personal use of campaign contributions, is unethical. The 73 senators and 191 representatives elected before 1980 can keep surplus funds when they leave office, although the representatives must retire before January 1993 in order to qualify for the loophole. Excess campaign contributions to them give the appearance of thinly disguised bribes. Currently, influential congressmen build retirement funds, in addition to their generous pensions, thanks to influence-buying PACs who contribute with the knowledge that the official is not likely to be seriously challenged in future elections.

The largest retirement withdrawal so far was by Missouri Representative Gene Taylor, who kept $345,000 of surplus funds when he left Congress in 1990. If the elected federal official dies in office, the money goes tax-free to the official's heirs. The estate of Alabama Representative William Nichols, who died in 1988, received $438,561 in leftover campaign donations.

Among recently retiring members of the House of Representatives, Georgia Congressman Doug Barnard stated that he had not decided whether to keep all of this $550,000 in accumulated campaign funds but that he might keep the 45 percent earned by "prudent management"—investment—of excess campaign funds. Barnard, a member of the House Banking Committee, received $179,512 from financial industry PACs during 1989–90. Representative Robert Whittaker of Kansas planned to donate his balance of $524,000 to his alma mater, the University of Kansas.

Even if the lucky congressmen do not retire by 1993, they can continue to use the accumulated campaign surplus for political purposes, including donations to others and their own future campaigns, as well as for the kinds of nonpolitical purposes described earlier. A Los Angeles city councilman was given permission by the state Fair Political Practices Commission to use campaign funds to hire a historian to help the councilman write a book about his political career.

Candidates running unopposed or with weak opposition should adjust their campaign fund-raising effort and expenditures accordingly. The *Los Angeles Times* reported that 60 percent of the $145.8 million spent by candidates for Congress in 1989–90 was spent by incumbents who ran unopposed or faced no serious challenge. That money was either wasted or used in the hope that it had built up a political advantage for future years.[31]

There is no legitimate reason to raise huge sums of money when the candidate knows a large surplus will result. Candidates do so either to build a campaign war chest that will deter meaningful opposition or because the ability to distribute a surplus to other candidates, for example, will increase their own power and influence. By the end of 1989, Minnesota

Senator Rudy Boschwitz had $5.3 million on hand, enough to discourage former Vice President Walter Mondale from challenging him. Later he raised yet another $2 million but was upset by Paul Wellstone, who made the senator's campaign finances an issue in the race.

Perhaps candidates should be allowed to raise as much money as possible, even though they expect a large surplus, because they would rather be safe than sorry. They naturally feel more secure with ample reserves. The press secretary for a congressman who usually runs unopposed said, "It makes sense to prepare for the possibility of a real race. If you have to go on television, what one day may look like a sizable war chest could be quickly depleted."[32] Politics is so unpredictable that there might be a last-minute need in a crisis that would make fund raising chancier. However, that tactic should be permitted only if the candidate pledges to return the excess to contributors on a pro rata basis.

ETHICAL GUIDELINES

1. Candidates for public office should divorce themselves as much as possible from the process of raising campaign funds. No candidate should ever pressure contributors by threatening retaliation or the withholding of legitimate governmental action. At a minimum, candidates should expressly state that no donation will cause them, if elected, to take any action that they do not independently believe to be correct. No candidate should permit any campaign staffer or aide to promise or suggest otherwise.

2. Elected officials must ensure that campaign contributors do not receive access to the official or the official's staff that is substantially greater than would be accorded to any constituent. No contributor should receive the benefit of any information that is not publicly known.

3. Candidates and elected officials have a duty to seek fair and equitable campaign financing reform that minimizes the inherent power of incumbents.

4. Candidates should not use personal or family wealth to substantially outspend opponents who rely primarily on contributions, although a reasonable disparity in such spending is justified when the opponent is an incumbent.

5. Candidates should not accept donations from a PAC or political party that are made in lieu of a direct donation from an individual, a business, a union, or another PAC if that direct donation would have been a political liability if publicized.

6. Candidates should not accept contributions in either "hard" or "soft" money from individuals, businesses, or unions that are subject to oversight or regulation in which the candidate reasonably expects to be directly involved. For example, it is an unacceptable conflict of interest

for a member of a legislative banking committee to take campaign contributions from the banking industry.

7. Public officials should not use excess campaign funds or their own PACs to contribute to other candidates or PACs. Public officials who control PACs are guilty of the appearance of impropriety because there is no legitimate reason for such control.

8. Candidates should publicly disclose accurate lists of all contributors and all expenditures as frequently as possible during a campaign, and this disclosure policy should include the last few days before the election. A final report should be made as soon as possible after the election, in addition to all other reports required by law.

9. Candidates should do everything possible to avoid campaign debt that persists after the election. They should not borrow campaign funds unless there is a reasonable expectation that all loans and bills can be paid with funds raised prior to the election.

10. Candidates should not continue raising campaign funds when it is apparent that a substantial surplus will result.

11. Candidates should return all surplus campaign funds to contributors on a pro rata basis. They should never convert surplus campaign funds to personal use, even if it is legal to do so.

NOTES

1. Chauvin, *Dollars Are Distorting the American Political Process*, 76 A.B.A.J., June 1990, at 8.

2. Schwartz, *Public Financing Riding High*, Wash. Post., Mar. 4, 1990, at A11.

3. *Preliminary Inquiry into Allegations Regarding Senators Cranston, De-Concini, Glenn, McCain, and Riegle, and Lincoln Savings and Loan, Open Session Hearings Before the Select Committee on Ethics, United States Senate, S.Hrg.No. 101–1190, Part 1*, 101st Cong., 2nd Sess., Nov. 15, 1990, at 2.

4. McGregory, *Keating, Cheating and Pols*, Wash. Post, Nov. 18, 1990, at C1.

5. Lauter, *Money Seen as Key Factor in Senate Choice*, L.A. Times, Nov. 8, 1990, at A1, col. 5.

6. Rohrlich, *Court Role in Initiatives Is Reasonable*, L.A. Times, Sept. 27, 1990, at A3, col. 5; Paddock, *Boost to Political Underdogs Seen*, L.A. Times, Sept. 27, 1990, at A3, col. 4.

7. ETHICAL OBLIGATIONS AND OPPORTUNITIES FOR ATTORNEYS GENERAL, Josephson Inst. Gov't Ethics Center, Dec. 1988, at 29.

8. Birnbaum, *Political Contributions of Narrow-Focus Groups Seen by Some as Growing Campaign Funds Issue*, Wall St. J., Dec. 22, 1989, at A8, col. 1.

9. *Id.*

10. Stewart, *Robert Dornan: A Master of Direct Mail*, L.A. Times, Oct. 28, 1990, at A20, col. 1.

11. T. O'Neill, MAN OF THE HOUSE 239 (1988).

12. Memorandum from Fred Wertheimer to Common Cause Members, Feb. 1990.

13. *Review and Outlook: The Haunted House*, Wall St. J., Nov. 11, 1988, at A10, col. 1.

14. 494 U.S. 652, 110 S.Ct. 1391, 108 L.Ed.2d 562 (1990).

15. Abranson, *Auto PAC's Spending Late in Campaign is Bane of Many Democratic Candidates*, Wall St. J., Nov. 2, 1990, at A16, col. 1.

16. Jackson, *Michel Joins Swelling Chorus of Republican Voices Calling for PAC Funding to Be Curbed or Ended*, Wall St. J., Dec. 5, 1988, at A12, col. 1.

17. George Washington Plunkitt, quoted in B. Jackson, HONEST GRAFT 95 (1988).

18. Birnbaum, *supra* note 8, at A8.

19. *Study Links Defense PACs and Key U.S. Legislators*, St. Louis Post-Dispatch, Mar. 18, 1990, at 7A, col. 3.

20. Bacon, *For Financial Firms Banking Reform Involves Huge Stakes—and Big Donations to Lawmakers*, Wall St. J., May 28, 1991, at A24, col. 1.

21. 421 U.S. 1, 96 S.Ct. 612, 46 L.Ed.2d 659 (1976).

22. Lynn, *Panel Criticizes Elections Board on Ethics Case*, N.Y. Times, Oct. 26, 1988, at B4, col. 1; *Campaign Financing Probed; State Ethics Panel to Begin Hearings*, Newsday, Jan. 18, 1988, at 6.

23. Jackson, *Cranston's Use of Voter-Registration Charities to Benefit Campaign Highlights Gray Legal Area*, Wall St. J., Mar. 1, 1990, at A18, col. 1.

24. GA. CODE ANN. 21–5–2 (1988).

25. Fritz & Morris, *Campaign Cash Takes a Detour*, L.A. Times, Oct. 28, 1990, at A1, col. 1.

26. Birnbaum, *supra* note 8, at A8.

27. Farney, *In Florida Governor Race, Lawton Chiles Runs Against Corrupting Influence of Money in Politics*, Wall St. J., June 29, 1990, at A12, col. 1; Reiss & Katel, *A Prescription for a Negative Campaign*, Newsweek, Apr. 30, 1990, at 22.

28. Reich, *California Election Insurance Commissioner: Garamendi Accepts Funds from Wives of Insurers*, L.A. Times, Oct. 29, 1990, at B3, col. 1.

29. Miller, *Lawmakers' Generous Alliance Unmatched in Congress*, L.A. Times, Nov. 2, 1990, at A35, col. 1.

30. GA. CODE ANN. 21–5–2 (1988).

31. *Campaign Cash Takes a Detour: House Incumbents Spend 65% of Their Election Funds on Items That Have Little Direct Link to Voters, a Times Study Shows*, L.A. Times, Oct. 28, 1990, at A1, col. 1.

32. Abramson, *In the Art of Politics: Fund-raising, Lawmakers' Arms Have Long Reach*, Wall St. J., Oct. 24, 1990, at A14, col. 2.

3

Campaigning

Adlai Stevenson (1900–1965) said, "The hardest thing about any political campaign is how to win without proving that you are unworthy of winning."[1] Assuming that campaign funds are collected ethically, the nature of the campaign itself must be examined. Should we expect a dirty, negative campaigner to suddenly adopt high standards of conduct upon election? In 1989, many who applauded President Bush's early ethics initiatives remained puzzled by the mean campaigning that had much to do with his 1988 election.

The increasingly sophisticated technology of instant polling and precisely targeted mailing and phone calls has turned political hit-and-run into an art form. A whole campaign can be orchestrated with unfair misstatements that inflame narrow groups of voters and move on to others before opponents can react. Markedly different media campaigns are created for different sets of voters. If opponents respond in kind, the mudslinging escalates.

High-minded political campaigns have not been characteristic of American political life. The 1988 presidential election illustrated the effectiveness of the new technology when both parties engaged in negative campaigning and deliberate distortion. While the Bush campaign was successfully making Massachusetts convict Willie Horton famous, Michael Dukakis dismissed a campaign aide who spread a rumor about Bush's alleged marital infidelity. During the primary season, Dukakis fired his chief campaign manager for circulating copies of the British politician's speech that was plagiarized by Senator Joseph Biden.

Political campaigns ought to be tough and hard-hitting, but only about issues, including ethics. The public needs to know if an opponent lies, cheats, or steals. As discussed in Chapter 11, even the private life of candidates may be relevant to their fitness for the job. But not every aspect of private or family life is fair game.

Candidates cannot control all the actions of supporters. Some may be tearing down opponents' posters while others make phone calls that destroy reputations. In 1796, supporters of Thomas Jefferson falsely accused John Adams of seeking to have George Washington removed from command of the Continental Army. Perhaps we have not changed much in two hundred years. Dirty tricks by underlings cannot be prevented, but a campaign that sets a high ethical tone from the top down will see less of them. The unfair tactics of Donald Segretti's team in the 1972 election included the so-called Canuck letter that was merely defamatory until it caused an emotional and rambling response by Ed Muskie that drove him from the race.

Richard Nixon's darker instincts may have been triggered by the dirty tricks against him in 1960—organized jeering, rotten eggs, and microphones cut off as he began to speak. In his 1962 California governor's race, Bob Haldeman engineered a mailing to Democrats from a fictitious Committee for the Preservation of the Democratic Party that claimed Pat Brown was a tool of left-wing extremists. Haldeman got caught, but the Nixon team refined its techniques over the next few years. The spirit of Dick Tuck, who arranged the legendary tricks against Nixon, lives on in a meaner form.

MEDIA, MAKEUP, AND MARKET SHARE

The expense of political technology drives campaign fundraising. So does the actual expense of campaigning through the mass media. Many campaign managers claim to allocate one-half of their expenditures for television. Political campaign mogul David Garth insists on reserving 75 percent of the total campaign budget for television.[2] A campaign budget is not the same thing as the total amount raised by the candidate. The average congressional candidate spent only 13 percent of his or her total funds on television ads. Even in close races, the cost of television was rarely more than 21 percent.[3] In 1988, $228 million was spent on political broadcast advertising, but that was only 8.4 percent of total political spending for the 1988 elections.

In statewide or national elections, broadcast advertising is more significant. In his 1986 election, both Senator Alan Cranston and his opponent spent more than one-half of their money on television and radio time. In the 1990 California gubernatorial race, the candidates spent a combined $20 million on television ads, about $13 per vote. Politicians can spend $500,000 on media buys in the last weeks of a campaign. Advertising can cause state or even some local campaigns to cost millions. Senate candidates spent an average of $3 million in 1988 races. A House seat cost about $360,000, three times the amount needed ten years ago. If we lived in small city-states like the Ancient Greeks or were governed by New England town hall meetings, massive media campaigning would be unnecessary. The reality is that modern campaigns depend on expensive media buys, marketing decisions, and candidate photogenics. Shallow, uninformed, but telegenic candidates win elections over substantive, effective officials who do not understand television. In *The Candidate*, Robert Redford portrayed a sincere, issues-oriented campaigner who was groomed to be a media star. After he won, he plaintively asked, "What do I do now?"

Today's equivalent of Harry Truman's whistle-stop campaign occurs when candidates fly from city to city, crossing a state or the nation in one day, touching down long enough for brief airport rallies or new conferences, the major goal of which is placing a sound bite on the local news. (The average sound bite shrank from 14.8 seconds in 1984 to 9 seconds in the 1988 campaign.) Until recently, candidates or their surrogates would address rallies or shake hands at factory gates, engaging in at least a limited form of traditional campaigning. Now, except for photo opportunities, those practices are virtually extinct.

The expense of paid advertising forces candidates to pick artificial, forced surroundings for good "visuals" to ensure that there will be free media coverage. Even if it were possible to ensure all legitimate candidates an equal amount of free time, we cannot constitutionally prevent candidates from buying additional air time.

What are the ethical implications of modern campaigning and the loss of significant direct contact between candidates and the voters? First, these things strengthen the influence of the special interest and PAC money that pays for the required technology and media exposure. Second, it subverts the ability of the candidates to compete fairly on the issues affecting their constituents.

If complex problems and solutions cannot be described in political shorthand, the most simplistic arguments may win. A dramatic example, even if ripped out of context, is more forceful than a cogent, complicated discussion of reality. In a 1966 election, an ad by New York Governor Nelson Rockefeller said of his opponent, Frank O'Conner, "If you want to keep the crime rates high, O'Conner is your man." Such a summary of a candidate's views on a number of law enforcement issues is impossible to rebut except by equally unfair retaliation in kind. One proposal in presidential campaigns is to provide free five-minute blocks of television time to encourage less simplistic and less negative advertising.

FAIRNESS

> Are you good folks aware that Senator Pepper is known all over Washington as a shameless extrovert? Not only that, but this man is reliably reported to practice nepotism with his sister-in-law and he has a sister who was once a thespian in New York City. Worst of all, it is an established fact that Mr. Pepper, before his marriage, habitually practiced celibacy.

If this famed attack by Senator George Smathers on then Senator Claude Pepper in 1950 were the worst example of political invective, there might be no unfairness to complain of. Other accounts of that election have Smathers accusing Pepper of being a "practicing homo sapiens" and a "sexagenarian."[4] Some uneducated voters may have been swayed by those charges. In 1968, a Democratic ad merely showed a picture of Republican vice presidential candidate Spiro T. Agnew, but the soundtrack was a man laughing hysterically. Should Joe Isuzu begin making political commercials, we might see equally outrageous but harmless political jousting. However, campaign tactics are frequently both outrageous and harmful. Political consultant Douglas Bailey recently said, "To get people's attention these days your TV ad needs to be bold and entertaining, and, more often than not, that means confrontational. And, unlike a few years ago, you don't even have to worry whether the ad is truthful."

It is often difficult to determine the source of the unfair ad. A blurb in small print may say, "Paid for by the Friends of. . . ." Alex Kroll, the chairman of the American Association of Advertising Agencies, urges a voluntary code of conduct requiring advertisers to clearly identify the sponsor of campaign ads and pledging to avoid innuendo or opponent bashing.[5] Tennessee Representative Bart Gordon proposed requiring television ads to show a photo of the sponsoring candidates that takes up one-third of the screen for four seconds, together with a statement that the candidate "takes *full* responsibility for the content of this advertisement."[6]

Ethically sensitive politicians need to know when they cross the boundary of fairness. Three 1989 elections in New York, New Jersey, and Virginia illustrate some of the problem in defining the boundary. In New York, ads run by Rudolph Giuliani emphasized David Dinkins's failure to file income taxes in the early 1970s. The ads were factually correct and raised an issue of competence and honesty, but they also suggested an ongoing problem without mentioning the length of time since those mistakes. In the Virginia gubernatorial race, both candidates ran highly emotional but inaccurate ads about the opponent's views on abortion, a complex issue about which no one's views can be accurately summarized in thirty or sixty seconds. Finally, the New Jersey gubernatorial race saw both candidates using the Pinnochio device of showing the opponent's nose lengthening while they spoke.

Texans have a lifetime supply of mud after their 1990 gubernatorial primaries and general election. In the primary, Ann Richards's opponent ran an ad that asked, without any supporting evidence, "Did she use marijuana, or something worse, like cocaine . . . not as a college kid but as a 47-year-old elected official sworn to uphold the law?"[7]

If unfair campaign tactics are unethical, there must be a way to measure unfairness in a way that voters understand. The only defense that a victim of unfair campaigning has, other than retaliation in kind, is to tell the voters why the charge or claim is unfair and expect them to punish the unfair campaigner. But voters will not reward a whiner—a candidate who complains about campaigning that is harsh but fair. For example, in the 1990 California Democratic gubernatorial primary, Diane Feinstein's opponent attacked her record as San Francisco's mayor, claiming that she left behind a $180 million deficit. Feinstein's overreaction, that the attack was like Richard Nixon's Red-baiting of Helen Gahagan Douglas in 1950, caused scornful editorials and slippage in the polls.[8]

Campaigning is unfair if it contains allegations that are untrue, defamatory, misleading to a reasonable person, or irrelevant to the legitimate qualifications for the office sought or to issues about which the electorate is legitimately concerned. (The term *legitimately concerned* is used because the electorate may be interested in private or confidential matters that are titillating but irrelevant to the candidate's views or qualifications.) The unfair campaigner rationalizes his behavior, thinking that the ends justify the means: "It is so important for the good of the [city/state/nation] that I, rather than my opponent, be elected, that negative, even dirty, campaigning is excusable."

Increasingly, newspapers are analyzing the fairness of political campaigning in every media. During the 1990 elections, the media effort to expose misleading ads seemed to reduce the number or excesses of negative campaigning. California's *Long Beach Press-Telegram* was a pioneer in this field. In 1984, it set up a hotline phone number two weeks before each local election to which readers could report sleazy campaign tactics. In addition to rebuking the candidates, the newspaper even withdrew an endorsement because of the candidate's improper tactics. The *San Francisco Chronicle*, along with other major metropolitan papers, began intense coverage of campaign advertising in recent years. In 1990, a Pete Wilson ad, referring to his service as Mayor of San Diego, quoted tax revolt guru Howard Jarvis as saying, "We wouldn't have needed Proposition 13 if everyone had run their cities like Pete Wilson." The *Chronicle* verified that Jarvis made that statement, but it also reported that when Wilson was mayor, he had opposed Proposition 13, an effort to cut property taxes.[9]

Newsweek described an ad by Senator Jesse Helms in which he referred to his 1990 opponent, Harvey Gantt, as "extremely different." *Newsweek*'s translation: He's black.[10] Frequently, the newspaper analyses of campaign ads are printed in "truth boxes," sidebar items that evaluate, line by line, the claims in an ad. The *Washington Post*'s "30-Second Politics" column shows still photographs from the commercial and exhaustively scrutinizes the text.

It is unfair to make deliberately false statements in campaign literature or speeches or to permit surrogates to do so. Candidates have an implied contract with the public to tell the truth. Jimmy Carter was a rare politician who formalized that contract by promising, "I'll never lie to you." Defamatory statements are also untrue, but, in addition, they damage an opponent's reputation or character. Misstating George Bush's position on housing is a false statement, but spreading lies about extramarital affairs is defamatory.

An oversimplification of issues or taking facts out of context is also unfair. The media does this when it summarizes a candidate's complete views. The time constraints on television reporting virtually forces oversimplification, although the media has a duty to be accurate. However, the candidate should always state the issues fairly. Some people can be confused or fooled with little effort, or even unintentionally. Intentionally misleading a reasonable person, the average voter, is unethical. It is the equivalent of lying. When planning for a hard-hitting sound bite or a one-liner for a debate, it is difficult to fully explain the ramifications, the pros and cons, of the complex issues in American life. But "quick and dirty" tactics will always get across to voters.

While media considerations encourage these tactics, they do not excuse them. It simply takes more effort to define and characterize complex issues so they can be easily understood. For example, subtle differences between candidates on the complicated choices to be made in the Middle East should not be glossed over with "My opponent is no friend of Israel, but I am." George Bush's campaign strategist, the late Lee Atwater, did an excellent if unfair job of making Willie Horton a symbol for Michael Dukakis's position on crime. (Atwater later apologized for those ads. He said, "it makes me sound racist, which I am not."[11]) The Democrats' response, which tried to link President Reagan to crimes committed by federal parolees, was an unsuccessful, unfair effort to retaliate.

Political ads are created by the same pitchmen who are expert in associating a product with images of prestige, success, or happiness. It is no surprise that most political ads try to convey feelings, rather than information. Long ago, James Harvey Robinson wrote, "Political campaigns are designedly made into emotional orgies which endeavor to distract attention from the real issues involved, and they actually paralyze what slight powers of celebration man can normally muster."[12] While feel-good ads are not unfair as part of an overall campaign strategy, they do not satisfy the duty of candidates to discuss the issues.

Senator Ernest "Fritz" Hollings has introduced legislation requiring the candidate to appear and speak in any ad that mentions opponents. Beyond raising First Amendment concerns, that approach may not solve the problem; more and more candidates seem willing to wield the knife themselves. Another bill, sponsored by Senators Daniel Inouye, Wendell Ford, and Warren Rudman, would impose a uniform format for all televised political ads less than ten minutes long prohibiting the use of actors, sophisticated visual devices (such as computer graphics), or off-screen announcers.

Finally, campaigners should not cloud the issues by raising questions about an opponent that are not relevant to his or her qualifications or judgment. Everyone has a skeleton in the closet or a black sheep in the family, and even unconventional virtue can be distorted. Until recently, personal matters like divorce were barriers to high elective office; Nelson Rockefeller is a well-remembered example. Presidents Johnson, Nixon, and Carter each had brothers who were embarrassments at times. And Betty Ford's refreshing candor complicated President Gerald Ford's political life. But do any of these cases reflect on the ability of the candidate to govern?

For example, is a candidate's brief, college-age experimentation with marijuana ever relevant to public office sought at a mature age? Attacks on Dan Quayle's National Guard experience were largely hypocritical, aside from the question of unfair family influence to get him in the Guard. Most college-age men with any option other than going to Vietnam took advantage of them. During Florida's 1990 Democratic gubernatorial primary, the fact that Lawton Chiles was taking a prescription antidepressant was leaked to the press. His opponent, Representative Bill Nelson, promised to release his own medical history, saying, "It has already been reported that I had treatment for hemorrhoids. Every intimate detail is a campaign issue."[13]

Candidates know when they launch an unfair attack. There is a campaign version of the Golden Rule: How would you feel if your opponent made a similar attack against you? If the answer is, "Terrible!" then the attack is unfair. Those are the charges and innuendo that will be relegated to a fifteen- or thirty-second advertisement because the candidate would not have the nerve to make them in a face-to-face meeting or a public debate.

Many voters instinctively feel the unfairness and if they are undecided, may vote for the victim. A 1990 *Wall Street Journal*/NBC News poll showed that two-thirds of the voters are bothered "a lot" by negative campaigns. Only rarely would a supporter change his vote because of disgust over his candidate's unfair tactics. Voters offended by negative campaigning may still vote for that campaigner because there is a clear choice in their minds—the other reasons to vote for him or her outweigh their distaste for the campaigner's tactics. The unethical campaigner may thereby be elected. The voters should find other ways to voice their displeasure.

An analysis of the 1990 elections by Thomas B. Rosenstiel of the *Los Angeles Times* concluded that candidates were adjusting to voter distaste for slick, negative campaigning by building ads around visual documentation, such as newspaper clippings and financial reports, and simplifying the photography and image techniques.[14] Several candidates began to deliver strong attacks against opponents on camera in person. The upset victory of Paul Wellstone over Senator Rudy Boschwitz resulted in part from a wickedly funny two-minute takeoff of the movie *Roger and Me*, titled "Where's Rudy?" It was shot like a home movie, showing Wellstone wandering around the incumbent's campaign headquarters and emphasizing his "outsider" status.

A candidate can legitimately argue that an unethical campaigner will be an unethical official. An "ends justifies the means" philosophy may be reflected in the elected official's job performance. The "dirty tricks" of Richard Nixon's campaigns resembled the "dirty tricks" of his administration in power. Breaking and entering at the Watergate resembled burglary at Daniel Ellsberg's psychiatrist's office. Although elected officials should be both competent and ethical, if we can choose between candidates of principle and candidates to whom expedience is most important, we ought to choose principle.

ACCESS

A candidate has a duty to be accessible to the press and the public on a regular basis and in an open setting. The political process at the national level has degenerated into a series of photo opportunities and speeches before controlled audiences. President Ronald Reagan's near total abandonment of press conferences may have been unique to him, but the trend is away from traditional campaigning in which real people met and questioned the candidates. Perhaps skill in choosing political handlers tells us something about the candidate, but not nearly enough. The public deserves to see candidates as they really are in public forums, in stressful situations, and working without a script.

During the 1988 presidential election, television showed Dan Quayle ambushed at his home by reporters shouting questions at him while he was taking out the trash. That may have looked like another abusive tactic by the press. What the public didn't know was that the Bush-Quayle organization had listed the trash dumping as the only time that day when Quayle would be available for questions.

Recent presidential campaigns involving incumbents were the low points in public appearance by candidates. Nixon's 1972 campaign and, to a lesser extent, Reagan's 1984 campaign reflected a deliberate strategy for the incumbent to appear "presidential" while using the power of incumbency and administration surrogates to do the work of campaigning. Carter's 1980 campaign was also conducted from the White House, but he had a slightly better excuse in the Iranian hostage crisis.

The fact that Harry Truman or Abraham Lincoln would fail miserably as contemporary media candidates demonstrates the triumph of image over substance. Modern campaigns for major statewide or national offices are not in the hands of the candidate. Rather, specialized political consultants like those in the movie *The Candidate* pick the issues and symbols and write the speeches. Their ideal candidate is a telegenic person who has no recorded views on anything and who is very coachable. They pick the issues and symbols based on overnight polling. They avoid spontaneity and the unpredictable at all costs. A *New Yorker* cartoon shows the political coach on the sidelines, sending in signals for moves such as "do a flip-flop," "oppose crime," and "wave the flag."

Candidates should meet in debates that explore issues in depth and test thinking ability rather than teleprompter skills. Real debates reveal strengths and weaknesses that slick ad campaigns gloss over. Real debates encourage the candidates to clash, rather than ducking questions from a panel while reciting mini–position papers. The theft by the Reagan 1980 campaign of President Carter's debate briefing book may have decided that election, but not because it tipped them off about Carter's position on the issues. Rather, it allowed Reagan to better prepare and deliver devastating one-liners like "There you go again!"

The front-runner, usually an incumbent, is always reluctant to debate. Why risk it? Most "debates" today are really candidate forums in which the candidates deliver set speeches, with little time for questioning by opponents or the press. Those forums are almost worthless when several candidates share the stage because there is no way to follow up on one candidate's view on one issue. It gets lost in the confusion.

The 1988 presidential and vice presidential debates were designed to be mere joint press conferences. CBS News wisely chose to not participate in the second presidential debate. The few direct exchanges between the candidates were exciting and revealing but violated the rules agreed to by the candidates' handlers to prevent such exchanges. To paraphrase

Senator Lloyd Bentsen's put-down of then Senator Quayle, "You're no Jack Kennedy," we can say to all phony political debaters, "You're no Lincoln or Douglas."

ELECTION DAY

The rule in Chicago was "Vote early and often." LBJ's first Senate victory was won with the help of voters who had been in the grave for some time. Even today, votes may be collected with walking-around money distributed on election day. Big city political machines get out the vote for candidates who make large donations to the machine for which it is not required to account. For example, a candidate may pay $10,000 to $20,000 to have his or her name placed on the sample ballot given to all voters on their way in to vote by poll watchers representing the machine. The realistic expectation is that most voters will follow the sample ballot exactly. In addition, candidates pay the machine for supporting get-out-the-vote services, such as providing rides to the polls.

The justification for these practices is both rational and patronizing. The argument is that, unlike affluent, suburban voters or yuppies, inner-city residents are less able to follow complicated issues and make informed judgments, so they delegate that work to their leaders in the machine. They are satisfied that those leaders will endorse candidates who are in the best interests of their followers. Even when the voters know or suspect that their leaders may be pocketing most of the candidates' money, they do not object because it is deserved for all the work they do protecting the voters' interests. Furthermore, if others are influenced by newspaper editorials or syndicated columns, what is wrong with loyal machine followers being influenced by the machine?

Finally, while the affluent can volunteer for election day activities, the less affluent need to be paid for the work they do on election day. A South Philadelphia ward leader said, "If you want us to push extra hard for you, put people on the street, we need extra money. You hire door-knockers, a housewife, you're going to give that lady $20 for her four hours work. If that's wrong, well, it's wrong."[15] Is it wrong? The answer is that fair pay for legitimate election day activities, including printing literature or voting cards and paying poll workers, is ethical. However, the "consulting fees" paid to machine leaders are bribes to influence the voters who rely on them for guidance. Period. There is little or no accounting for the money demanded by the local machine. A practical politician recognizes that there is no other way to get that vote, but an ethical politician must be troubled by the system that operates untouched in many urban areas. Only the most corrupt organization would support candidates whose views diametrically oppose the best interests of the machine's constituents. But the typical machine will support its natural candidate much more vigorously when the candidate pays for support and services.

ETHICAL GUIDELINES

1. Candidates for public office should publicly promise to conduct ethical campaigns, conforming to these standards at a minimum. They should do their best to ensure that campaign staff and supporters will also conduct themselves in an ethical manner and will discipline or dismiss those who do not.

2. Candidates should not permit "dirty tricks" or mean-spirited pranks that confuse or harass opponents. Even in hard-fought campaigns candidates should make every effort to remain personally cordial with opponents and their supporters.

3. Candidates should campaign only on the substance of legitimate issues affecting the electorate. Campaigns should focus more on the positive aspects of the candidate's positions than on the negative aspects of the opponent's views or actions. Facts regarding an opponent's private or family life should never be mentioned, unless there is a legitimate reason that such a fact reflects on the opponent's qualifications for office.

4. Candidates should not make statements that are misleading to reasonable people or rely on issues that are irrelevant to an opponent's qualifications for the office or to the legitimate issues affecting the electorate. This is a definition of unfair campaign tactics. A candidate's staff or supporters may not engage in any campaign tactic that would be unfair if done directly by the candidate.

5. Candidates are under a continuing duty of candor. If they make statements that they believe to be accurate or fair at the time but later learn have been false or misleading, they should promptly correct such statements or misimpressions. Candidates should try to ensure that corrections are publicized as widely as the original statements.

6. Candidates who feel that they are victims of an unfair campaign tactic should not retaliate in kind. Rather, they should explain to the voters in clear, plain language why the opponent is guilty of unethical conduct and let the voters decide whether their claim is correct.

7. Candidates have a duty to make themselves available to the press and public for open, candid exchanges, subject only to legitimate security concerns. Candidates, whether incumbent or not, who appear only in stage-managed formats unfairly deprive voters of the chance to question them directly.

8. Candidates should seek frequent, public encounters with opponents in which issues can be debated in reasonably unstructured settings. Subject only to generous time limits, candidates should be encouraged to

explore issues in detail in debates in which they may be challenged by opponents, the press, and the public.

9. Candidates should not pay money or give anything of value to other politicians in return for an endorsement or a promise not to work against the candidate. Campaigns can pay legitimate out-of-pocket expenses for necessary campaign expenditures, so long as political leaders are not enriched thereby.

10. Candidates should not pay money or give anything of value to a voter directly or to a third party when the candidate knows or suspects that the third party will pay voters.

NOTES

1. *Ethical Obligations and Opportunities for Attorneys General*, Josephson Inst. Gov't. Ethics Center, Dec. 1988, at 29.

2. *Quest for Campaign Money is Never-Ending in New York*, N.Y. Times, Mar. 21, 1988, at B1, col. 2.

3. *Campaign Cash Takes a Detour: House Incumbents Spend 65% of Their Election Funds on Items That Have Little Direct Link to Voters, a Times Study Shows*, L.A. Times, Oct. 28, 1990, at A1, col. 1.

4. M. S. Forbes, *Fact and Comment: With All Thy Getting, Get Understanding*, Forbes, Oct. 31, 1988, at 17.

5. Lipman, *Agencies to Attack Negative Political Ads*, Wall St. J., May 17, 1991, at A1, col. 1.

6. Bradley, *Gordon Wants "Mudslingers" Known*, Gannett News Service, Apr. 25, 1990.

7. *A New Era of Attack Politics*, Newsweek, Apr. 23, 1990, at 21.

8. *What Wilson Says in His New TV Ad*, San Fran. Chronicle, Apr. 23, 1990, at A7.

9. *Fighting Negative Ads with . . . Negative Ads*, Newsweek, Sept. 24, 1990, at 30.

10. Kibbe, *Atwater's Libertarian Legacy*, Wall St. J., Apr. 3, 1991, at A20, col. 3.

11. Reiss & Katel, *A Prescription for a Negative Campaign*, Newsweek, Apr. 30, 1990, at 22.

12. POLITICAL QUOTATIONS 147 (D. Baker ed. 1990).

13. Farney, *Strong Anti-Politician Sentiment Is Displayed in Poll Showing Deep Pessimism by Electorate*, Wall St. J., Oct. 26, 1990, at A16, col. 1.

14. Anthony Lewis, *The Intimidated Press*, N.Y. Review, Jan. 19, 1987, at 27.

15. P. M. Barrett, *Campaign Practices in Judges' Elections Spark Drive for Merit Appointments in Pennsylvania*, Wall St. J., Dec. 9, 1988, at A16.

4

Elected Officials

Unethical conduct by elected officials draws the most attention, even though elected officials represent a much smaller group than appointed officials or the vast pool of career government employees. We begin by repeating the belief that most elected officials are honest and competent, despite Henry Kissinger's comment: "Ninety percent of the politicians give the other ten percent a bad name."[1] By running for office, candidates not only implicitly promise to tell the truth, they also implicitly promise to fulfill their duties honestly. Many candidates also make those pledges explicit.

Americans think we know elected officials better than appointed officials or anonymous bureaucrats, and we are more disappointed when they fail. Although a healthy skepticism about government is an American trait, outright distrust is increasing. A 1990 Harris poll revealed that only 15 percent of Americans expressed a "great deal" of confidence in Congress, compared to 28 percent in 1984. In a *Wall Street Journal*/NBC News poll, 71 percent of the respondents said that the ethical accusations against the Keating Five would typify the behavior of senators and representatives.[2] The Keating Five's defense was that their conduct was not substantially different from any of their colleagues, consistent with the testimony of several of their colleagues. A *New Yorker* cartoon showed a politician kneeling by his bed, praying, "Please don't let it become the Keating *Six*." Someone suggested a better name: the Keating 535.[3]

The inherent temptations of public office may cause a person to act in ways that could not have been predicted. Like the old joke, if you'll do for a million dollars that which you won't do for a thousand, "we've established what you are; now we're only haggling about the price."[4] An elected official may suddenly find individuals or companies who are willing to pay the price. The argument that an honest person will act honestly in every situation may be true about absolutely honest people, who never compromise principle or justify and rationalize their conduct. Few such people exist in government or any other walk of life.

The nineteenth century political observer Mr. Dooley said, "The trouble with the House of Politics is that it is occupied by human beins. If 'twas a vacant house it would easily be kept clean." American government is structured in ways that reduce our reliance on the moral character of political leaders. In a dictatorship or monarchy, the people are entirely at the mercy of their leaders. The boast that we are a nation of laws, not of men, means that we can protect ourselves from the most corrupt and preserve civil liberty. However, most examples of unethical conduct are not so disloyal to the people as to be treason. Rather, most represent petty corruption by small gifts and favors. Minor compromises and rationalizations that are individually insignificant but damaging taken together are the real concerns of citizens. Therefore, this book is less about changing laws than about changing people's ethical attitudes and conduct.

Popular psychology says that an adult's basic character is fixed; we cannot change people. If a person with a latent character defect assumes a position of power and prestige, it is too late to remedy the defect. However, by creating an atmosphere in which ethics are valued and clear statements about proper conduct encouraged, we may deter public officials from improper actions. A public that has repeatedly endorsed high standards of conduct will be less forgiving and more likely to punish unethical officials. Dr. Martin Luther King, Jr., argued for the 1964 Civil Rights Act by stating, "Morality can't be legislated, but behavior can be regulated. Judicial decrees may not change the heart, but they can restrain the heartless."[5]

VOTING CONSCIENCE OR CONSTITUENTS

Former Iowa Senator John C. Culver faced this choice at the height of protests against the Vietnam War when Congress was to vote on a law making it a serious federal crime to burn an American flag. Although his constituents overwhelmingly favored the law, he voted against it as a matter of conscience. The freedom to burn the flag was an unpopular freedom, but Culver saw a more important principle at issue—in the long run, free speech and political protest should be protected, not restricted. That issue returned again in 1989, when Nebraska Senator Bob Kerry, a

Vietnam War hero, was one of the few to challenge the wisdom of such laws.

Our form of government permits rather lengthy terms of service, up to six years for senators, so that officials need not be swayed by day-to-day public pressure. Even where there is a power to recall state or local officials, the complexity of that process ensures that it will only succeed when an official has offended a large percentage of the electorate for a long time. *The Federalist* No. 10 declares that the legislative branch is designed to "refine and enlarge the public views by passing them through the medium of a chosen body of citizens, whose wisdom may best discern the true interest of their country and whose patriotism and love of justice will be least likely to sacrifice it to temporary or partial considerations."[6]

Elections in this country are not votes on specific issues, except for California-variety ballot propositions. Rather, they are for the purpose of electing people deemed qualified to make decisions on the constituents' behalf. Thomas Jefferson believed that elected representatives should respond immediately to the momentary majority, rather than exercising independent judgment or a long-term view. However, our system is closer to that reflected in the ideas of Edmund Burke, who thought that elected representatives should refine public opinion and act as the people would act if they were always wise.

The two leading views of a legislator's duty to deliberate and legislate are the delegate theory and the trustee theory. The delegate is elected to literally represent the constituents. In the event of a conflict between the legislator's conscience and the wishes of the constituents, the delegate votes as the constituents demand.

When U.S. senators were elected by state legislatures, rather than by the voters directly, the delegate point of view was called the "doctrine of instruction." An 1838 *Manual of Political Ethics* poked fun at this doctrine by suggesting that an official elected by a 2 to 1 margin should speak for two hours in favor of a law and then speak for one hour against it.

The trustee is concerned with the overall institutional values of society and protecting the individual rights of constituents. Over the long run, those goals ought to serve the constituents' best interests, but the trustee will choose conscience over the constituents' immediate wishes.

Philosophers have thoroughly explored the different aspects of those two views, including the questions about whether constituents really know what is best for themselves. And, as with whistle-blowers, a legislator's conscience may be over- or underdeveloped, reliable or unreliable. There are different levels of constituent need and preference to which legislators may respond differently. And who are the constituents? A majority of the population contained in the legislator's district, a majority of those eligible to vote or who actually voted, or a majority of those who voted for the legislator? Within the constituency, however defined, there will not be unanimity, and on some issues there may be no majority, but only a plurality. How does the legislator choose which position to adopt?

The philosophical questions are interesting and endless. The more practical ethical questions seem somewhat simpler. Candidates ought to promise in advance how they will resolve that dilemma. Will they always be delegates, mere instruments of opinion, or will they always be trustees, indifferent to polls and looking toward the long-term interests of the constituents as they understand those interests to be? Obviously, the problem is more complex because most candidates are willing to be mere delegates on some issues, but not on others.

A candidate might say, "I will follow the wishes of the majority of the voters in this district on almost all issues, but let me make it clear that I will never vote in favor of capital punishment under any circumstance." The voters may then elect that candidate for other reasons, even though most of them are in favor of capital punishment. For other candidates, the moral issues may be abortion, pornography, or nuclear arms, while on most taxing and spending issues they are content to implement constituents' wishes. After the election, the official must then uphold the promise. A North Carolina congressman who unexpectedly begins voting against tobacco interests because of conscience will be villified and certainly not reelected. However, if the voters were warned that he would do that if elected, they cannot claim that he deceived them.

A candidate may reserve the right to vote his or her conscience on certain issues without specifying in advance what those occasions might be. In the South, that's called buying a pig in a poke. You may be surprised at what you bought, but you're not surprised that you're surprised. Again, the electorate may be willing to vote for the maverick because they trust his judgment.

Teddy Roosevelt's description of the presidency as a "bully pulpit" applies to all public offices. Officials can shape public opinion rather than merely hire pollsters to detect it. There are times when a leader must lead, not follow. In the 1950s, almost all Southern congressmen publicly defended segregation and opposed all civil rights and voting rights bills, including several who were personally opposed to segregation. They justified their public posture by the argument that if they wanted to stay in office and do as much good as possible, they had to oppose integration because their constituents did.

Officials have a duty to educate and inform constituents so that public opinion will be based on accurate information and fair assumptions. They have a duty to lead public opinion on the ethical standards that should be required of public officials.

ACCESS

The public's right of access to the official does not end with the election. While any official interested in reelection will keep in touch with the folks back home, orchestrated media appearances do not give constituents a chance to confront, question, and argue with their representative. Even if the official is not interested in reelection or has lost a primary and is a lame duck, the right of access remains. We cannot re-create the politics of years ago when officials could visit around the courthouse square until everyone went home. But there should be a modern version of that style of politicking to ensure that the official knows firsthand what the electorate is thinking. Polling is an inferior substitute. Elected officials should hold open forums in communities across the district or state to talk with citizens about issues important to them.

Citizens should have access to elected officials and their staffs even if they did not support the official's campaign. While it is natural to prefer a known supporter, all citizens have equal rights to make their views known or to request assistance in dealing with bureaucratic problems. Former Minnesota Senator Rudy Boschwitz sold access to his office by creating two clubs of donors. Those who gave $1,000 or more got ten blue stamps that they could place on mail to the Senator; such mail would then get preference over nondonor mail. Contributors who gave less got stamps with different markings.

Senator Alan Cranston admitted, "A person who makes a contribution has a better chance to get access than someone who does not."[7] A former California state senator, Paul Carpenter, was convicted on federal corruption charges following the undisputed evidence and Carpenter's candid testimony that contributors get better access. The government's theory was that it was illegal for Carpenter to use his influence on behalf of a contributor's legislative proposal when he would not do so for others who did not contribute to his campaign fund.[8] That theory has been demolished by a 1991 Supreme Court decision, *McCormick v. United States*, in which Justice Byron White wrote:

Serving constituents and supporting legislation that will benefit the district and individuals and groups therein is the everyday business of a legislator. It is also true that campaigns must be run and financed. Money is constantly being solicited on behalf of candidates, who run on platforms and who claim support on the basis of their views and what they intend to do or have done. *Whatever ethical considerations and appearances may indicate*, to hold that legislators commit the

federal crime of extortion when they act for the benefit of constituents or support
legislation furthering the interests of some of their constituents, shortly before or
after campaign contributions, is an unrealistic assessment of what Congress could
have meant by making it a crime to obtain property from another, with his consent,
"under color of official right." To hold otherwise would open to prosecution not
only conduct that in a very real sense is unavoidable so long as election campaigns
are financed by private contributions or expenditures, as they have been from the
beginning of the Nation.[9]

Presidents are the politicians most likely to be isolated by the nature
of the office, the breadth of the constituency, and security concerns. But
a President who tried to overcome those obstacles and communicate
directly with voters as often as possible would surely be a more successful
President. Down the pyramid of elective offices to city councils and county
commissions, politicians cannot hide behind media advisers or scripted
interviews. They see constituents daily in stores and coffee shops and are
better representatives for it.

It has been said that we live under a government of men and women
and morning newspapers. Elected officials should make themselves available to the press on a reasonable basis, including holding frequent news
conferences when it is impractical to speak to numerous reporters individually. The press has the resources to follow stories and connect events,
some of which may not be publicly known, in order to find the facts.

Officials should cooperate with press inquiries and respond with the
same honesty and candor that they owe to the public itself. "No comment" is justified only when there is a matter of legitimate confidentiality.
Lies to the press are justified only in those extremely narrow circumstances when lies to the public are justified—temporary matters of national
security. Officials who abuse the national security excuse to conceal illegal
or politically motivated misconduct, as in the Iran-Contra affair, abuse
the public trust.

Cooperation with the press does not require officials to volunteer everything they know. In fact, volunteering information through leaks is unethical if the purpose of the leak is to unfairly attack opponents or violate
duties of secrecy. However, if an issue is of such public concern that the
press pursues it, the press should be treated as a surrogate for the public's
right to know. When the press is unfair or fails to report all it should, the
official is entitled to complain and look for alternate ways to circulate the
true story. But even an unfair press cannot be ignored or deceived merely
because doing so serves the official's interest, rather than the public's.

CONFLICTS OF INTEREST

Thomas Jefferson once received a gift from a Baltimore merchant. He
returned it with a note: "It is the law, sacred to me while in public

character, to receive nothing which bears a pecuniary value. This is necessary to the confidence of my country, it is necessary as an example for its benefit, and necessary to the tranquility of my own mind."

Contrast Jefferson's attitude with the experiences of a former Tennessee congressman, Bill Boner, who was given a 5 percent interest in an $18 million South Carolina hotel project for $5 and another 5 percent interest in a Virginia restaurant and motel for $50. The House Ethics Committee staff determined that both transactions were investments, not gifts. A cable television franchise expert said of the boom time for granting cable franchises, "If you wanted your application to be seriously considered, you would be expected to give an equity share to the right people, coinciding very precisely with the principal contending political factions."[10] Congressman Dan Rostenkowski made more than $50,000 in eighteen months from a $200 investment in a real estate development that he benefitted by his influence. *Wall Street Journal* reporter Brooks Jackson's book *Honest Graft* contains numerous examples illustrating the opportunities that can be pursued by public officials interested in increasing personal wealth while in public life.[11]

The conflicts of interest faced by elected officials have been classed as either unavoidable or avoidable. James C. Kirby supervised a 1970 Report by the Special Committee on Congressional Ethics of the Association of the Bar of the City of New York. He listed three types of unavoidable conflicts. First, there are inherent conflicts. Elected officials are likely to be parents, homeowners, taxpayers, and members of an occupational group such as lawyers or businesspersons. They could not recuse themselves from all decisions affecting those broad groups to which they belong. But the danger of misconduct caused by the conflict of interest is slight because the official's interest is also the interest of so many others.

One inherent conflict of interest was treated differently by the California Fair Political Practices Commission. A member of the California Coastal Commission, which has broad powers over development near the coast, was disqualified from voting on a hotly contested proposed sewer for Malibu because she lived in the sewer district. Along with 2,700 other homeowners, she would have been assessed more than $9,000 if it had been approved.[12]

Second, there are politically dictated conflicts. A farmer from an agricultural state will be representing his own interests when he acts as a delegate representing his constituents. Although he benefits from voting in favor or agriculture, his constituents do, also. Again, the potential for impropriety is slight because that conduct is highly visible and promotes widely shared interests.

Third, there are personally necessary conflicts. When the city council is not a full-time job, it is necessary for council members to have other employment. While the insurance saleswoman should not sell insurance to the city, there are numerous ways in which her interests as a small businesswoman will be affected by council action. There is also the conflict arising from the fact that time spent on business means that less time will be spent on council work. Personally necessary conflicts may present tough choices, but they are unavoidable.

All other conflicts of interest are avoidable. The ethics charges against former House Speaker Jim Wright were a laundry list of what to avoid: misuse of official influence by interceding with federal agencies on behalf of Texas energy and savings and loan interests that were major campaign donors; rent-free use of a Fort Worth apartment owned by the family of a former business partner; financial questions surrounding his book, *Reflections of a Public Man*; and business interests jointly owned with a real estate developer who also once employed the Speaker's wife. (The real estate developer might have profited from development of Forth Worth's stockyards resulting from large federal grants obtained by the Speaker.) His blind trust even owned a used Cadillac that according to Brooks Jackson "has been navigated through gaps in disclosure rules like a stealth bomber."[13] Yet by all accounts, Congressman Wright lived modestly and valued public service over personal wealth.

Lyndon Johnson's use of power and influence to obtain and protect his family's Austin television station license received some attention at the time. Today, it would be a fatal political mistake for a prominent politician to so blatantly line his pocket. More commonly, the public official puts himself in a position in which his or her debt or outside business interests threaten the exercise of independent judgment. Both the debt and the conflicting business interests can be avoided. The inadequate pay may encourage officials to cut corners in search of additional income, but that is no excuse. Public officials are given power over people. Therefore, it is fair to demand higher standards of conduct than may be found in other occupations.

Recently, Federal Express provided a jet to fly key members of the House Ways and Means Committee back to Washington so they could wrap up a tax bill—which contained a vital tax break for Federal Express. Senator Lloyd Bentsen formed a monthly breakfast group of lobbyists who paid $10,000 for the privilege. He later abolished the group. Former House Democratic Whip Tony Coelho entertained party contributors on a yacht and a Learjet belonging to a later defunct Texas savings and loan after lobbying for a bailout of the savings and loan industry.[14] In New Mexico, a private prison corporation bought forty acres of land on which to build a women's prison from a group of local officials that included a state senator who helped persuade the legislature to award the prison contract to the corporation. The land was sold for $3,500 per acre in an area where land sells for $250 to $1,500 per acre.[15]

The demands of raising huge sums of money for campaign finance, discussed in Chapter 2, create the most obvious conflicts of interest. The government relations director for the New Jersey Chamber of Commerce said, "In the past 15 years, I have not seen legislators who could be bought, but I met a lot who could be rented, who can be influenced by the need to finance their campaigns."[16]

There are an infinite number of unreported favors, direct and indirect, that may influence public officials. That is not to say that a public official is consciously abdicating the duty to exercise independent judgment. Either the chance of subconscious influence or the appearance of impropriety is a sufficient reason to forbid all avoidable conflicts of interest. In hindsight, Senator John McCain probably regrets the free annual family vacations at Charles Keating's palatial home in the Bahamas that ended in 1987.

Congress is not bound by the conflict of interest law that makes it a crime for an executive branch employee to take government action in which the executive or his or her immediate family has a financial interest, in the absence of an approved waiver. That crime is punished by a maximum of two years in prison and a $10,000 fine. Therefore, Senator Ernest Hollings did nothing illegal when he helped postpone the licensing of rural cellular telephone franchises while owning stock in a cellular phone company valued at $100,000. Senator Hollings said that he ordered the stock to be sold when he learned that his broker had bought it.

The President's Commission on Federal Ethics Law Reform recommended extending the conflict of interest law to include officers and employees of the judiciary and Congress, but not to representatives or senators themselves. The Commission's Report stated,

Although, in theory, the conflict of interest prohibitions should apply equally to personnel in all three branches of government, we were confronted with insurmountable practical problems in applying such general limitations to Members of Congress themselves. Particularly in regard to the votes they cast on the floor of each house of Congress, legislators are far less likely than personnel in the executive and judicial branch to be involved in a narrow range of matters in which they can reasonably be expected to hold no financial interests. Quite to the contrary, a Member of Congress participates personally and substantially in every matter that comes before his legislative body by simply voting on it. . . . .If [the law] were applied to Members of Congress, it would effectively require them to divest themselves of all private financial interests upon assuming office, or, alternatively, recuse themselves on a frequent basis, thereby leaving their constituencies without representation as to those matters.[17]

The same argument can be made about the President and state governors, as well as state legislators. The ethical response is that those officials should place all their possibly conflicting holdings in a blind trust, as discussed in Chapter 8. If the holdings are so small that a blind trust is impractical, it is unlikely that any actual conflict of interest will exist, and full disclosure will minimize the appearance of impropriety.

INDIRECT CONFLICTS OF INTEREST

There is a new trend in Congress to honor retiring members with fund-raising events to endow a home-state university chair in their name. Non-retiring members heavily solicit lobbyists, industries, and companies for substantial donations. For example, despite contribution limits and disclosure requirements for PACs, corporations were urged to give $25,000 each in honor of retiring Mississippi Senator John Stennis for such an endowment. A lobbyist who asked not to be identified said, "We operate in an imperfect world. And if I don't do this, my relationship with a member [of Congress] might be jeopardized. . . . That's pressure."[18]

Similarly, Dan Rostenkowski, Chairman of the House Ways and Means Committee, raised over three-quarters of a million dollars from corporations and unions to fund a bicentennial celebration of the committee. That paralleled Congress's raising of millions for its bicentennial. The big donors gave to both drives rather than face disapproval or lack of access to key lawmakers.

Conflicts of interest arise when an official's close friends or relatives receive a gift, contract, or job. Although the payoff is not made directly to the official, the actual influence or appearance of impropriety is just as great. A real estate developer who gives the mayor's husband a cushy, well-paid job accomplishes just as much as if he had paid the mayor directly. One of the charges against former Attorney General Ed Meese involved the hiring of his wife by an influence seeker. The Office of Government Ethics found that Meese repeatedly violated conflict of interest rules in dealings with or on behalf of E. Robert Wallach, his close friend and former attorney.

There is at least an appearance of impropriety when a politician's relative does business with the government that the politician serves. The husband of a Los Angeles County Supervisor continued to work on a $100,000 contract for the county after her election. Even though the work began before she became a Supervisor and she had no role in approving it, she recognized that the appearance was as important as the reality.[19]

Conflicts of interest rules should recognize that indirect conflicts are as damaging as direct conflicts. However, the friends or relatives are free agents who may not be dissuaded from accepting the gift, contract, or job. If the public official cannot prevent them from entering into that relationship with a person or business affected by the official's public duties, it should be disclosed promptly. The glare of publicity will minimize the danger that improper influence will result. New York Senator Alfonse D'Amato was "cleared" by the Senate Ethics Committee, which investigated the use by D'Amato's brother of the senator's office for a defense contractor client.[20] If that conduct could not have been prevented by the senator, it should have been promptly disclosed.

Potential conflicts of interest exist whenever a close relative works outside the home. Forty-five percent of congressional spouses hold outside jobs, ranging from teachers to lawyers and lobbyists. Those who are government employees are forbidden by the Hatch Act to campaign for their spouses. Marilyn Quayle took the position that she could not practice law while her husband was in public office. A few wives work in their husband's congressional office, even though the law prohibits them from being paid. Spouses with business interests involving prominent constituents or parties seeking political favors are scandals waiting to happen.

The working definition of "power couple" is Senator Bob Dole and Elizabeth Dole. Until she left the Cabinet, the Senate minority leader was married to the Secretary of Labor. If they had been from different parties, it would have made a good television sitcom. Texas Senator Phil Gramm is married to the chief of the Commodity Future Trading Commission, Wendy Gramm. When there was a key Senate vote on a regulatory issue, several senators thought that there was at least a potential impropriety. Former Senator William Proxmire said, "This is certainly a conflict of interest. Recusal would probably be a step in the right direction, but it still wouldn't remove the influence he would have."[21] When spouses, close relatives, or friends are on opposite sides of important governmental or policy matters, they should take reasonable steps to avoid actual conflicts of interest and the appearance of impropriety.

It is not uncommon for the children of legislators to become lobbyists, including children of the last two Speakers of the House, a former House majority leader, and Senator Dole's daughter. For the most part, they are sensitive to conflict of interest. However, in one case reported by the *Wall Street Journal*'s Jeffrey H. Birnbaum, the lobbyist son of Representative Sam Gibbons lobbied before the House Ways and Means Committee, on which his father sits, and approached his father individually on behalf of clients. At the same time, the son managed his father's campaign fund raising.[22] While both the father and son deny any improper influence, they were not sensitive to the appearance of impropriety.

It is a conflict of interest for an elected official to hold simultaneously a major post in a political party. Robert H. Jackson said, "Men are more often bribed by their loyalties and ambitions than by money."[23] While we expect partisan politicians to act as partisans, both the diversion of time from official duties and the temptation to use one power to reinforce another makes the official–party officer a special case. Recent New York City political scandals have a common thread of government decisions influenced by top-echelon party officials. New York Attorney General Robert Abrams said,

Allowing political party leaders to also hold public office creates an unhealthy accumulation of power in one individual. It was this sort of "one-stop-shopping" that led to Donald Manes having been dubbed the "King of Queens." Party leaders should be required to choose between their party post or a government position, but should not be allowed to hold both.

His concern recalls Lord Acton's famous epigram: "Power tends to corrupt, and absolute power corrupts absolutely. Great [powerful] men are almost always bad."[24]

HONORARIA AND FREEBIES

Public officials should not accept fees for speaking or merely appearing at events sponsored by groups seeking influence. Those fees, known as honoraria, are typically $1,000 to $2,000, in addition to travel expenses. It is not heavy lifting. Arkansas Representative Tommy Robinson received a $1,000 honorarium for touring Tyson Food's poultry plant.[25] In 1989, Representative Dan Rostenkowski received $285,000 in honoraria, although he gave more than 90 percent of his honoraria to charity. In later discussion Senator Christopher J. Dodd scolded his Senate colleagues:

Let's not delude ourselves. You are not being invited because you are a great orator, because you are Cicero. They are paying you $2,000 because they think you might listen to them. We must end the perception that the men and women who serve in this body have a price tag on them.[26]

In 1989, the House of Representatives gave us honoraria in exchange for two pay raises totaling almost 33 percent. Prior to reform, House members were limited to honoraria equal to 30 percent of their salary.[27] For senators, the limit was 27 percent. In the summer of 1991, the Senate finally went cold turkey on honoraria in exchange for a $23,200 pay raise.[28] Of the senators facing reelection in 1992, twenty-six voted against the honorarium ban–pay raise, while only seven voted for it. Executive branch employees are prohibited from accepting honoraria for speeches made in their official capacity.

The honoraria disease at its height led several companies and lobbyists to buy $2,000 worth of former House Speaker Wright's book in lieu of honoraria. (Wright's chief accuser, Representative Newt Gingrich, wrote a real book but then foolishly raised $5,000 each from twenty-one fat cats for a partnership to promote it. The partnership paid Mrs. Gingrich $11,500.) In 1987, the Chicago Board of Trade was under intense legislative scrutiny and paid honoraria of over $130,000 to members of Congress. When Senator Sam Nunn raised the "revolving door" question about Secretary of Defense nominee John Tower, who worked for defense industries after leaving the Senate, one reply was, "What about the $50,000-plus in honoraria you received last year?"[29]

Senators are permitted to donate $1,000 speaking or appearance fees to charity, a maneuver that barely lessens the impropriety. The group paying the honorarium ensures that the politician receives recognition from the charity that would not otherwise have been possible. However, the recent honorarium ban–pay raise did prohibit Senators from taking charitable tax deductions for such donations.

There is generally no regulation of honoraria at the state level. Prior to the passage of Proposition 73, California Assembly Speaker Willie Brown received $124,000 for sixty-three speeches in one year, as well as $40,000 in gifts that were legal because they were disclosed. An assemblywoman received a $10,000 speaking fee from the corrections employee group, ten times the fee normally paid by the group. She left the hospital shortly after surgery to vote for building a new prison, but she did not consider the honorarium as a reward for her vote.

California officials are now limited by Proposition 73 to honoraria of $1,000 per source per speech, in addition to travel expenses. Appearance fees, no matter how labeled, are inappropriate for public officials who receive full-time salaries. The President's Commission on Federal Ethics Law Reform recommended the abolition of all honoraria to federal officials.

There are sound reasons for public officials to speak at industry gatherings or be questioned by business executives. It helps keep them in touch with conditions in those industries and pays political dividends for the official. But the actual influence or the appearance of impropriety resulting from the payment of honoraria justifies eliminating them. In addition, allowing honoraria to flourish encourages excessive outside speeches and travel by officials who should spend that time and energy on official business.

A cousin to honoraria is the junket. Junkets consist of free travel without the job of speaking upon arrival. When the junkets are at government expense, the only ethical issue is whether public money is being wisely spent. Recently, a congressional delegation flew to France on military aircraft. The cost was $3,191 per person, compared to about $700 per person on a commercial airline. In 1985, Representative Bill Alexander flew to Brazil on an Air Force jet at a cost of $50,000. In 1989, one-fifth of the House of Representatives, plus aides, visited sixty locations around the world at a cost of over $1 million. While some members really do work constantly on those trips, other members are referred to as WCS, world-class shoppers.

However, when the junket is at the expense of private parties with business before the public official, there is a danger of improper influence and the certainty of improper appearance. A *Wall Street Journal* editorial stated that in 1987

12 of the 20 [Senate] Armed Services [Committee] members spent a total of 84 days at resorts, courtesy of private groups including defense contractors. [Senator Sam] Nunn and his wife spent 10 days in Honolulu, with round-trip airfare and two nights' lodging paid by Sea-Land Corp. of Elizabeth, N.J., which has a contract for carrying supplies to U.S. forces in Europe.[30]

Although the purpose of junkets is to give legislators firsthand exposure to subjects of legislative oversight, their value is open to question. Regardless of the answer to that question, when the junket is paid for by private persons or industries, public officials should decline the trip.

RUNNING FOR REELECTION

"How can a man serve the [public]? When out of office, his sole object is to attain it; and when he has attained it, his only anxiety is to keep it. In his unprincipled dread of losing his place he will readily go all lengths."
—Lun-yu, *Conversations and Sayings of Confucius,*
Recorded by His Disciples

The ethics of elected officials receive their sternest test as the officials plan for and enter reelection campaigns. In one sense, every politician is always running for the next election. But the temptation to abuse the powers of incumbency and collect campaign funds from lobbyists or special interests is greatest toward the end of the term. During 1989, the thirty-two Senators facing 1990 reelection campaigns were raising money at the rate of $145,000 per day. Georgia Representatives Newt Gingrich gave year-end bonuses to two staffers who had worked in his reelection campaign. He defended the bonus practice as common, although House rules prohibit payment of official staff salaries for campaign work.

Incumbents at both the state and federal level enjoy near 100 percent reelection rates. In California, incumbents won 97 percent of the Senate and Assembly races. In the 1990 congressional elections, 82 of the 405 House incumbents did not have an opponent from either national party, and another 300 had an opponent who raised less than $25,000. Only 23 races were really competitive. House incumbents raised $146 million, compared to only $24 million for challengers, and they also received at least $75 million worth of free mailings. Ninety-six percent of House incumbents were reelected. Only one incumbent senator was defeated in a year that saw the greatest number of Senate incumbents reelected since

1856. The loser, Rudy Boschwitz, spent $6.3 million against Paul Well-stone's $781,000, a differential that became the major issue in the race. As mentioned earlier, PACs love incumbents. In California, the 25 largest business PACs gave less than 3 percent to challengers. The rest of the $5 million they distributed went to incumbents.

Public officials running for reelection find it difficult to separate official decision making from the political needs of the campaign. Squeezing the last project from the pork barrel and making key personnel appointments are sure ways of winning votes. Senator Patrick Moynihan bragged to constituents that one magazine's reference to him as the "King of Pork" meant that he was successful in protecting New York interests. President Nixon insisted on questionable defense projects as part of a secret "Keep California Green" strategy to carry the state in the 1972 election.

The book *Showdown at Gucci Gulch* quotes Senator Alan Simpson's remarks about Alaska Senator Ted Stevens:

I have been here seven and a half years. I have watched with total admiration as the senator from Alaska does his work in the U.S. Senate. It should leave us all absolutely envious. Because I have seen him with his extraordinary skills insert more pieces of legislation into various bills for his state than any person that I have ever met in this place. I think the people of Alaska should be proud of that; that is why they return him here, only one of the reasons.

I have seen him work hard on the Appropriations Committee. I am not on the Appropriations Committee, but I have seen pieces of legislation come from that committee which were literally larded with material that had to do with the state of Alaska.

I am not going to get into one with the senator from Alaska because he is a pretty feisty cookie; but I can tell you if they wanted a bear to represent them in Alaska, they hired a grizzly. That is Ted Stevens.

I think that is great, but I do not think you can come in here and have a debate that has to do with talking about things and costs and so on, when I have seen things come here under the direction of the senator from Alaska which were of tremendous cost—railroads, unified commands. There is no limit to the extraordinary ways—he is the envy of us all.

I have seen him produce the most novel legislation. I have seen condition upon condition come from wherever this remarkable gentleman plies his trade, project after project, waiver after waiver.[31]

The power of incumbents to obtain jobs for constituents is the most important reason that voters choose incumbents. During the 1980s, the Hughes Aircraft Company built factories in the districts of six key members of congressional committees that control Hughes' business with the government. In the aerospace industry, that is referred to as "political diversification." If the cost of producing goods for the government is higher because of unnatural political diversification, scattering component manufacturing plants around the country, the taxpayer ultimately suffers.

The extensive use of the free printing and mailing privileges given Congress and available to all officials to some extent is employed most as reelection time rolls around. The federal "franking privilege" cost $113 million in 1988.[32] Congress ends more than 12,000 pieces of mail to constituents for every letter received from constituents. In 1990, the total was $62 million pieces of "franked" mail. Under new rules, senators can send statewide mailings six times a year. A recent reform effort, which included the requirement that such mailings be marked "mailed at taxpayer's expense," disappeared in a conference committee. The Chairman of the Commission on Congressional Mailing Standards, former Representative Morris Udall, said, "I have often been appalled by the way some Members have perverted the frank. There can be no doubt that by the use of slick, highly targeted mailings many Members have greatly increased their chances for re-election."

Constituent newsletters and routine correspondence are easily defensible. However, frequent mailings toward the end of a term with an ostensible public purpose are really efforts to raise name recognition one more notch. California's recent Proposition 73 banned all newsletters or mailings of more than two hundred pieces.

The use of legislative staffers to raise campaign money is an obvious abuse of the powers of incumbency, as well as a misuse of public resources. Commissioners and mayoral aides helped raise more than $700,000 for Los Angeles Mayor Tom Bradley over a five-year period. It is difficult to believe that those efforts did not involve a substantial use of city staff, offices, and equipment. A lobbyist representing Charles Keating brought $250,000 in checks for voter registration charities directly to Senator Cranston's Capitol office.[33]

There have been scattered legislative responses to this abuse. A recent Los Angeles ordinance prohibits the hand delivery of campaign contributions in city offices and prohibits local appointees from soliciting contributions from anyone until three months after a city agency renders a final decision in any matter affecting their interests. The new Florida campaign reform law prohibits fund raising in public buildings.

One unique power that the majority party has every ten years is the gerrymandering of legislative districts based on the latest census. The overriding but rarely mentioned issue in the 1990 elections was the power to draw districts. The use of creative geography to protect entrenched politicians, including incumbent members of the minority party, is a favor the members do each other. Detailed, block-by-block census maps and computer programs enable the party in charge of a state's redistricting to draw boundaries for congressional districts that will give it the best chance of capturing a maximum number of seats. In the thirteen states that lost population in the 1990 census, incumbents in the controlling party will protect one another, trying to erase the district represented by a member of the other party.

The power of incumbency has been reduced to a mathematical model by Emory University's Alan I. Abramowitz. He concludes that the most important factor in the closeness of an election is the challenger's campaign spending. The model predicts the margin of an incumbent's victory (or defeat) by quantifying the partisanship of the district (District), the incumbent's personal popularity (Personal), the incumbent's seniority (Senior), the type of committee the incumbent serves on (Comm), the incumbent's rate of defection from his or her party's position on roll call votes (Defect), the amount (Inc\$) and utility (Sqinc\$) of the incumbent's campaign spending, the amount (Chal\$) and utility (Sqchal\$) of the challenger's spending, the challenger's elected office-holding experience (Chelect), and the incumbent's party affiliation (Party). The resulting formula looks like this:

$$
\begin{aligned}
\text{Margin} = {} & a + b_1 \times \text{District} + b_2 \times \text{Personal} + b_3 \times \text{Senior} + b_4 \times \\
& \text{Freshman} + b_5 \times \text{Comm} + b_6 \times \text{Defect} + b_7 \times \text{Inc\$} + b_8 \\
& \times \text{Sqinc\$} + b_9 \times \text{Chal\$} + b_{10} \times \text{Sqchal\$} + b_{11} \times \text{Chelect} \\
& + b_{12} \times \text{Party}^{34}
\end{aligned}
$$

Or you could spend your time trying to win the lottery.

BRIBERY OR BUSINESS AS USUAL

> All bribes offered to members of legislative bodies, as indeed all bribes, may be classed under the heads of direct, indirect, and unconscious bribes. Direct bribes given by private individuals to legislators are now exceedingly rare, or perhaps do not occur at all, owing chiefly to the Argus-like press, to the dread of inevitable ruin should it ever be divulged, and to the great probability that some day or other the evil deed will transpire, and, once transpiring, will be most extensively known through the papers.
> —Francis Lieber, *Manual of Political Ethics* (1838)

A book about political ethics struggles with the danger of sounding like Pollyanna, unrealistic and naive. Politics is a process of give-and-take in which only compromise succeeds. However, the process of give-and-take raises ethical concerns when it impairs the independent judgment that officials owe to their constituents. The philosopher Barrows Dunham said that integrity is making up one's own mind according to principle. We know that a legislator who introduces a bill or votes for it in exchange for money commits the crime of bribery. What if he does the same thing in exchange for a legislative quid pro quo—"I'll vote for your bill if you'll vote for mine"?

Berkeley law professor and judge John T. Noonan is the author of *Bribes*, the ultimate treatise on bribery. Noonan defined a bribe as "an incumbent improperly influencing the performance of a public function meant to be gratuitously exercised."[35] While vote trading by legislators or similar acts of reciprocity by public officials are not likely to be prosecuted, that conduct satisfies the definition of bribery. One of Noonan's examples is Abraham Lincoln. Abraham Lincoln? Noonan cites the "logrolling" (vote trading) and patronage encouraged or directed by Lincoln in order to pass the revised Thirteenth Amendment, abolishing slavery. The Republican Senate leader, Thaddeus Stevens, said, "The greatest measure of the nineteenth century was passed by corruption, aided and abetted by the purest man in America."

When Congress wrote the 1976 Tax Reform Act, vote trading was rampant. In order to obtain favorable treatment by Representative Claude Pepper, then Chairman of the House Rules Committee, a "transition rule" was included, which read:

An exception from the repeal of authority to issue I.D.B.'s [Industrial Development Bonds] for convention centers would be provided for a specified amount of bonds issued for expansion of a convention center with respect to which a convention tax was upheld by a state supreme court on February 8, 1985.[36]

The only convention center that met that criterion was Miami's. The book *Showdown at Gucci Gulch*, by Jeffrey H. Birnbaum and Alan S. Murray, is full of other examples of vote trading for what was deemed a good legislative end.

Senator Alan Simpson's distaste for vote trading dates to his first days as a state legislator when he learned that the Wyoming Constitution provides, "If any member of the legislature shall give his vote . . . upon consideration that any other member will give . . . his vote, . . . he shall be deemed guilty of bribery."[37] Assuming that most instances of vote trading or reciprocity between public officials would not be viewed as criminal conduct, are they unethical? The principal harm to be avoided is the official's failure to exercise independent judgment. If the vote or action promised would have been rendered just the same based on the official's independent judgment, the only concern is the appearance of impropriety.

However, if the official would have voted or acted differently but for the offered reciprocity, his or her constituents or the public generally have been cheated. The justification for accepting the reciprocity is that, in the long run, constituents or the public will benefit. If a legislator trades a vote on a bill that has little effect on his or her constituents for the vote of another legislator on a bill with a substantial effect on those constituents, the legislator serves their interest. The value judgments and quantification of intangibles that such a justification requires are staggering.

The better approach is a firm principle: Public officials should always exercise independent judgment on each issue or decision that comes before them rather than to abdicate that judgment in exchange for the reciprocal promises of other officials. Legislators should not swap votes. Rather, they should promise themselves, their constituents, and their colleagues that they will vote on the basis of all available information, considering the best interests of their constituents and the public good.

TERM LIMITS

The recent interest in limiting the number of consecutive terms legislators can serve tells us that voters are ready to treat the symptom of unethical politicians, since they feel powerless to effect a cure. Three out of four Americans want to limit the terms of members of Congress. President Bush has endorsed the idea. His maximum term is already limited. The *Wall Street Journal* reported that the wife of one congressman approached former Representative Jim Coyne, Co-chairman of Americans to Limit Congressional Terms, and said, "You have to stop doing this! What else can my husband do? You're trying to take his job away!" Colorado, California, and Oklahoma have adopted term limits for state legislators. States may seek to limit the terms of their congressional representatives even if there is no uniform federal limit.

Term limits are neither ethically right or wrong. Ethical, efficient public officials should be entitled to serve as long as the voters wish. There are good practical arguments that removing the most experienced legislators will strengthen the executive branch. Political commentator Hodding Carter III argues that waves of fresh senators and representatives will never master the skills necessary to make the Defense Department and other bureaucracies accountable. Supporters of the limitations claim that the benefits of weakening the influence of special interests is worth the risk. Furthermore, term limits cut the public expense of the huge pensions that long-time legislators accumulate.

Term limits will not be effective without thorough campaign finance reform. The cost of campaigns would be at least as great, perhaps greater if neither candidate has good name recognition. Rather than expect to continue in office, incumbents nearing the end of their term will be even cozier with the special interests that will hire them when they are forced out. Even if term limits are accompanied by other reforms, elected officials need to follow a set of ethical standards even higher than those required by law.

ETHICAL GUIDELINES

1. Elected officials are bound by the same ethical guidelines as those that apply to all public officials and must constantly work to maintain and justify the public trust they have been given.

2. Elected officials must represent all the people in their district, regardless of whether they are voters or whether they supported the official. In addition, officials must act in ways that improve the entire government in which they work, as well as the nation generally.

3. If a candidate for office cannot in good conscience act in ways demanded by a majority of his or her constituents, voters should be clearly informed of that reservation, so they can evaluate the candidate accordingly. If an elected official confronts a conflict between conscience and the constituents' wishes, the official must act in a principled manner even if it causes political damage to the official.

4. In most matters, legislators should represent the majority view of constituents when it is possible to know that view. Otherwise, legislators should decide issues using their best judgment in light of what best promotes the interests of the constituents and society as a whole.

5. Public officials have a duty to lead public opinion by ensuring that constituents have access to good information and that they have the benefit of the officials' thinking. Officials should attempt to shape public opinion responsibly, rather than merely acting by rote as passive representatives of the public will.

6. Elected officials should be reasonably accessible to the public for the purpose of open debate, discussion, and questioning. Officials should welcome the chance to have open-ended meetings with people at which they can seek public input and explain their own views.

7. Elected officials should be reasonably accessible to the press and media, doing interviews and press conferences and cooperating with all legitimate press inquiries.

8. Elected officials are worthy of the public trust only when they are free from all avoidable conflicts of interest, whether financial, personal, or familial. If there is any doubt about whether a conflict of interest exists, the official should remember the need to avoid even the appearance of impropriety. Decisions made when the official is under an unavoidable conflict of interest should be made publicly and as the result of the official's best judgment.

9. Elected officials should ensure that influence seekers do not create a conflict of interest or the appearance of impropriety by doing favors for close friends or relatives of the official. If the elected official cannot prevent the friend or relative from accepting a gift, contract, or job from a person or business affected by the official's public duties, the official should promptly disclose the relationship.

10. Elected officials should refuse honoraria, speaking fees, or money of any kind from any source that may wish to influence their actions, except for appropriate travel expense reimbursement. However, they should refuse free trips or travel expense reimbursement for junkets or other events at which they do not speak or in cases in which the length or expense of the trip is out of proportion to the legitimate speaking engagement.

11. Elected officials should not hold a major position in a political party.

12. Officials who seek reelection should not solicit political contributions from those who will feel pressured to contribute by reason of the officials' actual or apparent power over them. Elected officials are bound by the ethical duties of all candidates in the raising and spending of campaign funds.

13. Elected officials should not use the privileges of their position to directly aid a reelection campaign. For example, an official who normally sends one newsletter per year to constituents at government expense should not increase the number of such mailings during a reelection year.

14. Public officials should always exercise independent judgment on each issue or decision that comes before them, rather than to abdicate that judgment in exchange for the reciprocal promises of other officials.

NOTES

1. *Congress*, Bus. Wk., Apr. 16, 1990, at 54.

2. Abramson, *Thrift Scandal, Viewed as Political Dynamite, Is Slow to Detonate*, Wall St. J., June 13, 1990, at A1, col. 1.

3. Abramson & Rogers, *The Keating 535: Five Are on the Grill, but Other Lawmakers Help Big Donors Too*, Wall St. J., Jan. 10, 1991, at A1, col. 1.

4. *The Foul Stench of Money*, Time, July 4, 1988, at 21.

5. POLITICAL QUOTATIONS 174 (Baker ed. 1990).

6. THE FEDERALIST 57 (Lodge ed. 1894).

7. Abramson & Rogers, *supra* note 3.

8. *Conviction Calls Capitol Practices into Doubt*, L.A. Times, Sept. 18, 1990, at A22, col. 1.

9. ___U.S.___, 111 S.Ct. 1807, 1816, 114 L.Ed.2d 307, 317 (1991). Emphasis added.

10. Tolchin, *Rewards of Public Service Are Growing*, N.Y. Times, May 13, 1990, at 4, col. 1.

11. B. Jackson, HONEST GRAFT: BIG MONEY AND THE AMERICAN POLITICAL PROCESS (1988).

12. Russell, *Malibu Sewer Victory May Be Short-Lived*, L.A. Times, Nov. 16, 1989, at J1, col. 2.

13. Jackson, *A Used Cadillac May Mean Trouble for Speaker Wright*, Wall St. J., Mar. 13, 1989, at A1, col. 3.

14. *The Foul Stench of Money*, *supra* note 4.

15. Tolchin, *supra* note 8.

16. Schluter, *Contributions Don't Affect Votes? Don't You Believe It*, Governing, Aug. 1990, at 98.

17. To Serve with Honor: Report of the President's Commission on Federal Ethics Law Reform, Mar. 1989, at 15.

18. Havemann, *Lawmakers Lobbying for Endowments: Positions Honor Stennis, Others*, Wash. Post, May 28, 1988, at A1.

19. *Husband of Molina Still in Business with County*, L.A. Times, May 21, at B1, col. 5.

20. McFadden, *Foes of D'Amato Say Inquiry Hurt His Re-Election Chance*, N.Y. Times, Aug. 4, 1991, at 21.

21. *Senate Feels Impact of Marriage as Gramms Push Through Markets Bill*, Wall St. J., Apr. 26, 1991, at 5A, col. 1.

22. Birnbaum, *Rep. Gibbons and His Lobbyist Son Form Team That's Cozy Even by Standards of Capitol Hill*, Wall St. J., Feb. 5, 1990, at A16, col. 1.

23. B. C. Forbes, *Thoughts on the Business Life*, Forbes, Oct. 16, 1989, at 308.

24. Political Quotations 174 (Baker ed. 1990).

25. *Moonlighting: They Used to Call It Constituent Services*, Common Cause Mag., July–Aug. 1989, at 24.

26. *Senators Vote to Cut Off Honorariums for Speeches*, L.A. Times, May 22, 1991, at A4, col. 5.

27. Birnbaum, *Congress May Push for New Restrictions on Outside Income Due to Wright's Book*, Wall St. J., June 17, 1988, at 50, col. 1.

28. Eaton, *Senate Votes Itself $23,200 Raise While Banning Honorariums*, L.A. Times, Jul. 25, 1991, at 1, col. 5.

29. *Review & Outlook*, Wall St. J., Feb. 28, 1989, at A20, col. 1.

30. *Id.*

31. J. Birnbaum & A. Murray, Showdown at Gucci Gulch 250–51 (1987).

32. Armstrong, *Campaign Unreform*, Wall St. J., June 8, 1990, at A20, col. 4.

33. Fritz & Morris, *Senators Tap War Chests for Public Purposes*, L.A. Times, Apr. 28, 1991, at A1, col. 2.

34. Abramowitz, *Incumbency, Campaign Spending, and the Decline of Competition in U.S. House Elections*, 53 J. Politics 34, 38 (1991).

35. J. Noonan, Bribes (1984).

36. Birnbaum & Murray, *supra* note 31, at 147.

37. Wyom. Const. art. III, § 42.

5

Appointed Officials

At all levels of government, more officials are appointed than elected. The appointive power is one of the chief tools of an elected politician. Frequently, the quality or ideology of a politician's past appointments is an issue in a political race. At the local level, a mayoral candidate may run against a board or commission appointed by the incumbent, as much as against the incumbent directly. Presidential candidates promise to ensure that Supreme Court nominees will be acceptable to certain major groups of supporters.

In addition to concerns about competence and ideology, appointed officials, like all public officials, experience ethical conflicts and choices. They frequently have more day-to-day contact with corrupting influences than the politician who appointed them. If a developer wants a zoning change, it is efficient to become close to several appointed members of the zoning commission. Otherwise, if the developer seeks to influence a zoning change primarily through contact with the mayor's office, pressure may filter down to the zoning commission in unpredictable ways.

Allegations about the Department of Housing and Urban Development (HUD) under Secretary Samuel Pierce follow a pattern of government grant programs awarded to political friends. A HUD deputy assistant secretary admitted taking $100,000 in cash and noncash payoffs, corrupted by "just downright power and greed."[1] Los Angeles Mayor Tom Bradley's staff, as well as his appointees on city commissions, ran his fundraising campaign from City Hall, using city telephones and postage meters.

The same employees and commissioners who collected campaign contributions were involved in city business with the contributors.

Appointed officials also face ethical conflicts caused by their relationship with the appointer—the elected official. Lawyers who represent corporations frequently must decide whether the real client is a corporate officer who hired the lawyers, the board who hired the officers, or the shareholders who really own the corporation. The correct answer is the shareholders. But it is difficult to make that choice when there is no effective way to communicate with the shareholders, and the officers or directors can easily fire the lawyer.

Similarly, appointed officials always remember who appointed them and who has the power to reappoint or remove them. Does the appointed official owe allegiance to the appointer, those who voted for the appointer, all voters, all taxpayers, or all citizens? The correct answer is all citizens. But appointees can rarely appeal directly to the public when they go against the wishes of the appointer.

Political friends of the appointer instinctively know how to influence the appointee. When a well-known friend of the governor requests that an appointed director of a state agency exercise discretion in enforcing or interpreting a rule, the friend need never mention the governor's name, much less threaten to use influence. It would be a breach of political etiquette to do so. When a President's aide writes a letter of introduction or makes an introductory phone call on behalf of a private party, the appointee does not need to be told explicitly, "This is our friend. See that he is treated right." The message is clear.

The ultimate check by the voters on the ethics of appointed officials is the power to vote out the appointer. An elected official who consistently makes bad personnel choices or improperly influences appointees deserves to be thrown out of office. However, that is at best a remote, indirect way to control the appointee. If the appointees' conduct is so egregious that it violates conflict of interest laws or other criminal laws, they might be prosecuted. But most unethical conduct does not fall in that category. The mechanism for removing high-level appointed officials is typically as cumbersome as that for impeaching elected officials, if one exists at all.

The overwhelming majority of appointed officials are honest, well-meaning people who are not looking for opportunities to be unethical or corrupt. However, they can engage in questionable conduct simply because they have not thought carefully about the special ethical duties they owe to the public and the need to approach governmental jobs differently than business jobs. A heightened sensitivity to ethical concerns and adherence to a comprehensive statement of ethics will be the only reinforcement that most appointees need.

LOYALTY TO THE APPOINTER

It is both natural and healthy that appointed officials have a strong sense of loyalty and gratitude to the person who appointed them. *Natural* because the appointment, whether or not actively sought, is a prestigious honor, a source of real pride. *Healthy* because to a certain extent the appointee ought to carry out the agenda of the elected appointer. It would be unhealthy if appointees did not, within ethical bounds, advance the ideas and campaign promises of the appointer. Feelings of loyalty will always exist if an identifiable person or persons had a substantial role in the appointment process. Even when a politician submits a short list of nominees, as for some judicial appointments, with the final selection made by an independent group or subject to legislative confirmation, the appointee knows whom to thank. The issue is the proper role of that loyalty in the course of the appointed official's duties.

The resolution of this problem begins with the elected officials, the appointers. They should make early, consistent public statements about the standards of ethical conduct they expect from their appointees, including a promise to avoid placing the appointees in awkward ethical positions. The politician who clearly takes that position can say to friends who are looking for favors from appointees, "Look, I'd like to call [the appointee] for you, but I've made it very clear that I won't interfere with her at all so long as she's doing her job."

Whether or not the politician takes that position publicly, appointees should secure a private promise that they will not be called on to do anything they feel to be unethical. There is a diplomatic way to do that without offending the politician: "Governor, I'm honored that you are considering me for this job. I hope I can meet your high standards, including your strong views about ethics. I know that you'll want me to tell you if I'm feeling political pressure to do something that's not right. You obviously want me to do what's right in this important office." Like the candidate with moral reservations about certain issues, prospective appointees can accept appointments subject to the appointer's agreement that they will never be called on to do certain things.

How those messages are delivered will depend on several factors, including the relationship between the politician and the appointee. However, no one should accept appointment to any public office unless he or she is reasonably secure from pressure to repay the favor of the appointment in any improper way.

Many appointed officials have experienced situations in which they disagreed with the appointer about whether a requested favor was proper or improper. The appointee may think that the requested action is an inappropriate political payoff. The elected official may see it as a legitimate need of a personal or political friend in an area where the appointee has discretion to act or take no action. Misunderstandings are inevitable. But more than a few conflicts of this kind indicate a serious problem. Either the agreement about ethics was not reached, or it has been breached.

It is also possible that the appointee's sense of ethics is too strict to operate in a political arena in which ethical calls are mostly shades of gray, rather than black and white choices. Appointees who view every contact with supporters of the appointer as ethical black and white will neither succeed nor enjoy themselves. The balancing act that appointed officials must maintain does not give them the luxury of ignoring political realities. Rather, they must ensure that those realities do not cross ethical lines—the consensus view of proper conduct that is reflected in a widely endorsed code of ethics.

TO FISH OR TO CUT BAIT

> The British Cabinet officer comes from Parliament and on resignation returns to it, so that he has an elected political status in principle no different from that of his leader. The American official on resigning loses not only his ministerial power but any public role. He does not explain his resignation in the House or retain a seat there, as did Churchill throughout most of his wilderness years. He becomes an instant outsider. Thus, the American officer rightly feels he is the President's servant.
> —Charles Fried, *Order and Law: Arguing the Reagan Revolution—*
> *A Firsthand Account* (1991)

When an appointed official refuses to engage in unethical conduct, but the appointer will not support the decision, it is time to choose. Does the appointee swallow the impropriety, accede to the demand, and hope that it will escape public attention? Does she quietly resign, giving the common, ambiguous reason, "to pursue other opportunities"? Or does she go public and draw attention to an unhealthy situation?

Resignations as a matter of conscience or principle over matters other than unethical conduct also raise ethical questions. Jerald F. terHorst was President Ford's first appointment, but he resigned as Press Secretary because of disagreement with the Nixon pardon. Cyrus Vance's resignation as Secretary of State over President Carter's decision to attempt a rescue of hostages in Iran is another example of principled conduct by an appointed official. Each case will be different, but there are a few basic guidelines for appointed officials who face these choices.

The decision to give in to the pressure and remain in the job can be justified by balancing the significance of the impropriety or policy matter against the long-term public good that can be accomplished if the ap-

pointee stays in office. Could Secretary Vance have done more good as
a persuasive voice on the inside, like Clark Clifford counseling President
Johnson on Vietnam? A more common ethical dilemma might be indirect
nepotism—the hiring of a relative by a political associate in an environment prohibiting direct nepotism. If a county executive is barred from
hiring his wife as his secretary, he may prevail on an appointed department
head who needs a secretary to hire her. Even if she is well qualified, the
job resulted from a form of nepotism. But if she is well qualified and failing
to do that favor would damage the appointee's effectiveness in the long
run, hiring her may be an acceptable choice. Of course, a continuing
series of small compromises may cumulatively raise an ethical red flag.
If the suggested impropriety is grave, such as a criminal violation, there
is no choice.

If the seriousness of the impropriety or policy disagreement and the
wisdom of remaining in office cannot be balanced, the appointee must
make the decision to resign or wait to be fired. In some appointive jobs,
firing is virtually impossible, but the official can be frozen out of government and his job made difficult. If the appointee issues a public statement
describing the impropriety but does not resign, he becomes a renegade.
An appointed official who digs in his heels and insists on being fired may
create valuable publicity, but like the official who is frozen out, his job
performance will suffer. If he resigned, a new appointee in that job would
be able to function better and may even be more protected from improper
pressure because of the public attention to the resignation. The official
should do what is best for the public, but that includes the possibility that
the publicity will focus on the appointer's views or practices.

A quiet resignation on principle may be justified by the loyalty owed
to the appointer. It may preserve the appointee's reputation in political
circles—"Well, they had a strong disagreement, but she's honest and has
guts." In another role or a later administration, that person may be called
on for even greater public service. The resignations of Attorney General
Elliot Richardson and Assistant Attorney General William Ruckelshous
during the height of Watergate, although not quiet under the circumstances, ensured their continuing reputation as men of great character.

Co-author Michael Cody resigned as Tennessee State Attorney General
in part because key legislators were upset with his advocacy of an ethics
legislation package and his involvement in a statewide public corruption
investigation of the bingo industry that led to the guilty pleas or convictions of about fifty people, including many politicians. In Tennessee, the
Supreme Court appoints the State Attorney General. Cody understood
that his continuance in office might lead to arbitrary budget limitations on
his office, as well as legislative difficulties for a major legislative proposal
that the Supreme Court, his appointer, was promoting. However, in public
statements about his resignation, he chose to remain silent on that issue

and emphasized the other major reason—that he could not financially continue in public service with the expense of children in college.

Resignation accompanied by a public statement calling attention to an impropriety or policy disagreement might also be known as "going down in flames." The flames burn bridges and may restrict future chances at public service. It is the kind of move to make only when the improprieties are extremely serious, and the appointee is absolutely sure the charges are accurate. On the other hand, if a great public outcry occurs and reform results, that resignation was the highest kind of public service, self-sacrifice.

ETHICAL GUIDELINES

1. Elected officials (appointers) should take all reasonable steps to ensure that appointed officials (appointees) are persons of good character who will be both competent and ethical. Appointers should publicly promise appointees the freedom to act according to their best judgment and without political interference, even when the appointer disagrees.

2. While appointees should demonstrate appropriate loyalty to the appointer, their primary loyalty must be to the public. Assisting the appointer's political agenda is appropriate if the requested action or inaction is otherwise proper and is consistent with the public interest.

3. Appointees should seek public office only for the opportunity to render public service, rather than for personal gain. Appointees should not accept an appointment to public office unless it is clear that they will have the freedom to act ethically without interference or retaliation by the appointer.

4. Appointees should resign from public office if the appointer places them in a situation in which the seriousness of a requested impropriety outweighs the benefit to the public of their continued service. If the impropriety is grossly unethical or criminal, the appointee should resign immediately upon learning of it. If a series of minor improprieties becomes cumulatively serious, the appointee should make it clear to the appointer that those improprieties must stop. If they continue, the appointee should resign.

5. Appointees who seriously disagree with a decision or policy of the appointer may choose to resign as a matter of principle. Appointees may ethically use the same process of balancing the seriousness of the disagreement or importance of the principle with the potential public good that may result if the appointee remains in office.

6. The appointee should resign quietly out of loyalty to the appointer unless the improprieties are individually or cumulatively so serious that the public deserves to know. The former appointee should assist in the

effort to correct or prevent the unethical conduct that caused the resignation.

7. Appointees should consider the political nature of most government jobs before accepting an appointment. If they are not comfortable giving appropriate access or consideration to the appointer's friends or supporters, they should decline the appointment or make their position clear to the appointer.

NOTE

1. *Former HUD Official Tells House Panel How Public Job Led to Private Success*, Wall St. J., July 31, 1989, at 12, col. 1.

Public Employees

Most of the work of government is done by career civil servants, not elected or appointed officials. The federal government alone employs more than three million people. Most civil servants work in fairly low-paying, unglamorous jobs. From the army of clerk-typists needed by government agencies to highly skilled, dangerous frontline police and fire-fighting jobs, the traditions of civil service typify the best aspects of life in a democracy. American civil servants report to supervisors in agencies and to elected officials, but their ultimate responsibility, like that of all officials, is to the public. The pressures of serving multiple masters adds to the difficulty of their roles.

There is no doubt that the vast majority of civil servants are both competent and honest. As with other professions whose ethics have been publicly examined, the examples of misconduct come from only a few. The allegations of corruption in the Food and Drug Administration by employees who blocked drug approvals in exchange for bribes is shocking because it appears to be so isolated. However, broader ethical issues that do not involve dishonesty also affect civil servants. Should civil servants unionize? Whether or not they unionize, should they strike? To what extent should they lobby or campaign with lawmakers or the public for better wages or working conditions? Should they be involved directly in political campaigns?

Historically, the treatment of civil servants lags behind the treatment of workers in competitive private industry. However, government continues to attract employees because civil servants are also shielded from many of the pressures facing workers in the private sector. Other than in the most highly skilled positions, from which industry can "steal" public employees, most civil servants prefer the stable, calm, and secure atmosphere of a government office. By definition, the primary motivation for most civil servants is not money. For police or fire fighters, there are virtually no other outlets for their overriding interest in helping people, to "serve and protect." They have less bargaining power to improve their pay and working conditions because they have only a limited market for their skills.

The public interest in efficient government is at risk if civil servants are complacent or unproductive. How do you balance the inability to pay market wages with the public pressure for the same productivity expected in private business? In Chapter 8 we deal with the issue of fair pay for public service. It is relevant here if any civil servant uses low pay/no future as an excuse for laziness, theft, or unjustified walkouts. Government employees face the increasing threat that some jobs may be privatized, that is, contracted to private firms that prove they can provide better service for less money. Unethical behavior by civil servants is less likely to attract publicity or investigation than similar behavior by high-ranking elected or appointed officials. The petty corrupting influences on civil servants are less dramatic but cumulatively may be far more damaging to the public. No reporter will win a Pulitzer Prize for revealing the small gifts received by county purchasing agents or the free meals for cops on the beat. However, those small favors become perks, and businesses that refuse to play the game may be treated unfairly.

Government executives, agency heads, mayors, and governors should regularly recognize good civil servants. Because it is unlikely that pay rates will ever be sufficient in themselves to retain the best public employees, government must find other ways to reward them. Public recognition is one of the best. Small bonuses for cost-saving or efficiency ideas are also useful. Most importantly, every level of government should have consistent, fair, and frequent evaluations of civil servants that reinforce good feelings and provide genuine help to employees who need to improve. If the written record of those evaluations is necessarily public documents, the supervisor should exercise discretion about including all the constructive criticism that might be given orally.

THE SAFE HARBOR OF CIVIL SERVICE

The protections of civil service principally shelter public employees from the whims or political pressures of elected or appointed officials. Civil service employees can work without fear of direct political retribution, since they can be fired or demoted only for cause. Thus, an election board employee can act in a nonpartisan manner without fear of firing. A policeman can arrest the mayor's drunk son without worrying about his pension.

However, civil service protection is not absolute. The ethical policeman may be assigned to the graveyard shift. A politician disappointed by a departmental employee's action can use indirect influence on the employee or the entire department. A city council or legislature holds the purse strings for the whole agency. That knowledge is an institutional pressure on government employees to avoid tough calls or seek less stringent remedies, rather than cause political offense. At some point, only public pressure can restrain the indirect use of power over civil servants, but those who publicly complain take the same risks as other whistle-blowers.

Another defect of the civil service system is that, especially at lower governmental levels, it does not cover public employees who should be free from political influence. In some cities and counties, entire staffs of valuable employees serve at the pleasure of elected officials. The officials who want to retain their patronage power argue that the need to provide superior service to the public (so they can be reelected) justifies the at-will employment of staff. Obviously, these unprotected employees are much more likely to favor the official's campaign contributors and friends.

In a 1990 decision, the Supreme Court held that patronage was unconstitutional, an infringement of the First Amendment rights of job seekers who did not do political work for the incumbent.[1] The lawsuit was brought in Illinois, a state where the Republican governor and the Republican Party controlled more than sixty thousand state jobs. (The Democrats may control thirty thousand in Cook County.) The five plaintiffs claimed that they were denied promotion, layoff recalls, or hiring because they were not Republican. Applicants for state jobs were required to be registered Republicans and have written recommendations from local party leaders.

In New York City, 30 percent of the city work force, or forty-five thousand jobs, are in discretionary (patronage) positions. Patronage impairs the judgment of employees who wish to keep their jobs or receive promotions by continuing to be politically loyal, and, by ignoring merit selection, patronage may prevent the hiring of the best-qualified employees. Whistle-blowing is virtually not existent among patronage employees. At the same time, the patronage system is defended because the delivery of efficient city services by a motivated bureaucracy is better than by a purely civil service bureaucracy. Patronage is so ingrained in politics, especially at the local level, that the Supreme Court decision will be difficult to enforce if political hiring is done with any degree of subtlety.

The tension between the need for public employee job security and the requirement that employees be productive and efficient exists both in the civil service system and outside it. The need to hold all public employees to the highest standards of public service ethics does not depend on how the employee is classified. Unethical conduct by public employees should always be sufficient cause for discipline, including dismissal. The procedural safeguards of the civil service system will ensure that the discipline is consistent with the seriousness of the ethical breech. Public employees outside the system who are disciplined for unethical conduct may be subject to more arbitrary treatment. However, no public employee should be fired or demoted for acting in an ethical manner, even if they are at-will employees who, by acting ethically, have failed to advance a political interest.

WHISTLE-BLOWING

> If you are going to sin, sin against God, but not against the bureaucracy—God will forgive you, the bureaucracy never will.
> —Admiral Hyman Rickover[2]

Public employees should always present grievances, complaints, and reports of misconduct to their supervisor or through other designated channels. If the system investigates and corrects the problem, the employees have fulfilled their duty. However, if the system fails to make a good-faith effort to investigate and correct the problem or if there is retaliation against the employee, the employee has a further duty.

After using all available means for working within the system, unless it is futile to do so, the employee may be required to report the problem to other governmental agencies or to the public or press directly. That is known as whistle-blowing. Whistle-blowers told us about $7,400 coffee makers and a $2 billion cost overrun on the C–5A cargo plane. Two public interest groups wrote a booklet entitled *Courage Without Martyrdom: A Survival Guide for Whistleblowers*.

Whistle-blowers are not automatically heroes. Americans don't like tattle-tales. There is limited protection for whistle-blowing federal employees, but virtually none for state or local employees. Both the complaint and the whistle-blower's sincerity must be evident before the public will pay much attention. The desire for revenge, fame, or recognition is not a legitimate reason for whistle-blowing. We are also skeptical of whistle-blowers who claim to act out of conscience; we know people with overactive consciences, those who see unethical conduct where most people see the normal give-and-take of life.

There are two broad kinds of cases in which whistle-blowing may be justified. First, the agency or an official is violating the law or engaging in serious unethical conduct. Second, the employee has been pressured or required to violate the law or engage in serious unethical conduct or has been punished for refusing to do so. In the first case, an employee might discover that critical specifications in government contracting have been ignored or that an official is on the take. If the agency will not take action, the employee should notify law enforcement authorities. Unless the conduct created a problem affecting public safety, there is no need for the employee to go public, placing herself or her job in greater jeopardy. In addition, public discussion at that stage might compromise law enforcement's ability to investigate.

Only if law enforcement seems to be covering up the problem further would the employee be justified in seeking publicity. If the police or prosecutors have not pursued the employee's allegations because there seems to be no factual or legal basis for the claim, the whistle-blower may be liable for defamation or may face discipline for insubordination. Even if the whistle-blower is proven correct, overt and subtle retaliation may last for a long time. The tribulations of Pentagon analyst Ernest Fitzgerald, who blew the whistle on sloppy contracting practices and massive cost overruns, demonstrate that a whistle-blower is not without honor save in his own agency.

The second category of whistle-blowing cases occurs when public employees are punished for acting ethically. For example, a constituent or friend of the supervisor or elected official requests a favor that the employee would not normally perform for other citizens. After the requested favor is refused, the official learns of it and orders the employee to comply. If the employee refuses to do so, the official may have another employee render the service. Then, the employee finds his workload increasing, his coffee breaks disappearing, his raise denied, or a host of small inconveniences for not being a team player.

If the employee is fired outright, the case is clearer. If there is no effective civil service protection, the employee may quietly seek another job and walk away. However, if the employee was the victim of illegal conduct or a pattern of serious ethical abuse by an agency official, the public needs to know. Their right to honest, efficient government is being violated. The press may help investigate and publicize the unhealthy situation.

Increasing attention is being given to a federal statute dating back to the Civil War that puts some teeth into whistle-blowing about economic crimes. The False Claims Act was revised in 1986 and makes government employees, as well as other citizens, private attorney generals with the power to sue companies that defraud the government. The financial incentive to do so exists because the citizen receives 15 to 30 percent of the treble (triple) damages collected by the government.[3] Congressman Howard Berman predicts that there will be over $1 billion in recoveries within a few years under the act. One appellate court recently expanded the incentive by removing the defense that a government agency knew about or tolerated cost overruns and other problems. In 1987, California passed its own False Claims Act.[4]

Whistle-blowers should be protected by law and granted anonymity. However, when the whistle can be traced to a small office or handful of employees, the legal protection may be wishful thinking. The federal whistle-blower law in the Civil Service Reform Act was amended in 1989, but it contains many exemptions for particular agencies and does not excuse the release of confidential information as part of the whistle-blowing, making whistle-blowing illegal when it necessarily involves confidential matters. The ethical duty on the part of the public employee is the same, even if legal protection of their employment is not perfect.

UNIONS

A common view of unionization in the private sector, even among management, is that unions only come into businesses that have failed to treat employees fairly—not lavishly, just fairly. New Japanese industries in the United States place great emphasis on building a family spirit and loyalty, both to enhance productivity and to deter unionization. As American management becomes more responsive to workers' needs, beyond just better pay, the role of unions declines.

That same cycle has played out in the public sector. The unmistakably shabby treatment of civil servants has led to the formation of public employee unions. The existing public employee unions tend to be less militant than other industrial unions. That restraint is caused partially by the conflicting feelings of public employees who do not feel naturally comfortable in union activity but who join as a last resort. Because the ultimate power of any union is job action, public service–minded people, like teachers or police, are reluctant to aid the reduction of public service.

As with private sector unions, the need for them should diminish if the employer, government, is more responsive to workers' needs. Again, those needs include many more concerns than higher pay. In fact, higher pay is often demanded by public employee unions to make up for other adverse conditions that could be corrected more cheaply.

Union activity by public employees would be unethical if motivated by a desire to gain an advantage over the public. If strikes or threats of strikes were due to outrageous demands for above-market pay or freedom from all pressures to be productive, that conduct would be unethical, even if it were legal. However, most public employee job actions are motivated by governmental mistreatment of debatable but not outrageous demands. In 1991, about one-third of Montana's state employees went on strike seeking a raise of sixty cents per hour. Their last raise had been 2.5 percent in 1989, following a four-year wage freeze.[5] No one argued that they were paid well, much less overpaid.

It is widely accepted that certain categories of public employees, such as members of the military, have no right to strike. Organized or unorganized employee protest that threatens national security or the public welfare is improper. President Reagan's 1981 firing of 11,400 air traffic controllers reaffirmed that principle.

Labor mediator Theodore W. Kheel said that the controllers were

working for the government, under a law—good or bad—that made a strike against the United States Government an "illegal act," and providing that, if you struck against the government, you could never work for the government again—that was the law the President enforced. And a lot of people thought the law was cruel. But there it was.

As a lawyer, I was asked during the strike: "Do you oppose the President?" He had no choice![6]

Any strike or other job action by public employees alarms the public. It is the only time most taxpayers experience the same feelings of anger and confusion that management feels when facing a strike or walkout in the private sector. However, the public reaction is rarely justified. Strikes or slowdowns by most public employees do not threaten the vital functions of government, although they may be annoying. If caused by legitimate grievances, undertaken with restraint, and modified if serious public interests are endangered, such actions are not unethical.

A harder case arises if the strike becomes so prolonged that vital functions of government are threatened. A strike by sanitation workers is merely annoying, unless huge quantities of uncollected garbage cause disease or infestation that impairs public health. At the same time, the strike threat would be hollow if the public knew that the employees would stay out for only two weeks. Strikes are effective because they may last indefinitely. In the sanitation workers' strike, an ethically balanced response is to resume collection services for restaurants or hospitals, where the public health problem is greatest, but to continue the strike for residential or office trash.

The hardest case of all is the strike or slowdown by police or fire departments, whose work is always a vital governmental service. Other than writing fewer parking tickets or ignoring nonessential forms, no police functions can be curtailed without a serious threat to public safety. Generally, fire departments have no functions other than fighting fires and conducting inspections. Their dilemma recalls Mark Twain's story about the old lady in poor health who had no bad habits she could stop in order to improve her situation: "She was like a sinking ship with no freight to throw overboard." Public employees whose job actions automatically threaten the public interest have the least bargaining power of all.

The conclusion is not especially satisfying, but it is at least evenhanded: It is unethical for public employees to engage in a strike or slowdown that endangers public health or safety. And it is unethical for taxpayers or public officials to allow pay or working conditions to be so inadequate that reasonable, conscientious public employees feel the need to take such actions.

POLITICS AND PUBLIC EMPLOYEES

Part of the compact we have with civil servants that attempts to free them from political pressure also limits their freedom to be politically active. The federal version, the Hatch Act, has become a model for other levels of government. It prohibits employees from being partisan candidates in national, state, or local elections or taking an active part in political campaigns. Employees are forbidden to be involved in political fund raising, soliciting votes for or against a candidate, or appearing in a political advertisement. In 1990, Congress passed revisions of the Hatch Act that would allow political involvement, except fund raising, during nonworking hours and permit federal employees to run for office within political parties, but not for partisan political office. President Bush vetoed the bill.[7]

We want citizens to be treated equally by public employees regardless of the political ties of either the citizen or the employee. We want public employees to do the public's work on the public's time, not to be campaigning. We want agency heads and politicians to pressure all employees to be productive, rather than rewarding those who backed the right horse. In short, although we have a highly political form of government, we want public services delivered in a nonpartisan manner. Even when politicians have patronage power, they should not permit employees to mistreat citizens who supported an opponent.

Public employees should be able to raise concerns about governmental activities or working conditions with appropriate officials or lawmakers. However, they should not engage in political deals in return for favorable treatment. If the police benevolent association endorses a mayoral candidate, it is betting that the candidate will win and, if so, will favor the demands of the police over other city employees. Like other campaign donors, public employee unions that contribute money to political campaigns seek special access and consideration after the election. Given the limited resources available to address the needs of all public employees, officials should be free of political pressure to favor one group over others. Government at every level should distribute pay raises and benefits proportionately among all employees, allowing for different skills and risks.

Public employees cannot have the best of both worlds. If their jobs are basically secure from political pressure, they should forego the benefits of political activity. They should be informed about public affairs and should vote. They should be active in civic groups or broad-based consumer or environmental pursuits. If a local office or referendum is truly nonpartisan, the dangers of public employee involvement are minimal. However, the danger remains if an employee of one level of government actively participates in the politics of another level. For example, it is difficult to separate issues and interests when a state employee actively supports partisan candidates in either local or national elections. Even if that employee intends to conduct his job in a nonpartisan fashion, there is an appearance of impropriety, a fear by political opponents that politics will seep through.

A CODE OF ETHICS FOR PUBLIC EMPLOYEES

Public employees have many responsibilities in common with private employees. Although they are not striving for profits, they are striving for the same productivity and efficiency that would create profits in business, but which in public service are used to increase services or lower taxes in the public sector. A concise statement of ethics for public employees could be built around a set of duties owed to different groups: customers, taxpayers, other government agencies and employees, agency executives, and politicians.

The generalized version that is included in this chapter's "Ethical Guidelines" could be customized for particular agencies or offices. Each agency or department should discuss and adopt a similar statement. That process accomplishes two goals: (1) it heightens employees' sensitivity to ethical issues and helps convince them they work in an ethical environment and (2) it gives them more specific guidance than "be honest, do good."

The code of ethics will be least effective if imposed from the top down. Unilateral expressions of utopian views by agency executives or politicians looking for good publicity will not trickle down to the employees facing hard choices—not even if such slogans are framed and hung on the wall. The process of adopting or discussing an ethics statement will not be quick and easy. One could adopt the Golden Rule in a few minutes, but only without discussion of its specific applications. At regular meetings or a special retreat of the entire staff, the code can be discussed, amended, and adopted. Remember that the agency head or supervisor is probably not the best person to lead those sessions. An outsider or a qualified, sensitive discussion leader may be a better choice.

The Josephson Institute, an ethics foundation in Los Angeles, relies on three strategies for effective ethics training that will help increase employees' ethical awareness. First, increase ethical *consciousness* by suggesting the ways in which ethical issues arise and how they are decided.

Remind everyone that each person has ethical instincts and values that should be consciously used at work, also. Second, increase ethical *commitment* by causing employees to promise themselves privately and each other publicly that they will use their personal values on the job. They will be publicly acknowledging the impact they have on others, including the public generally. Finally, increase ethical *competencies* by discussing real or hypothetical examples that cause employees to think step-by-step through ethical dilemmas and identify the advantages and disadvantages of different choices. We may do right instinctively, but we will do right more consistently when we have a pattern for ethical decision making.

ETHICAL GUIDELINES

1. Public employees who are neither elected nor appointed should be given reasonable job security with dismissal, demotion, or other discipline only for cause or financial exigency. *Cause* includes unethical behavior, including job-related violations of law or breaches of a code of ethics adopted by the relevant office or agency. Employees should not be fired or demoted because their ethical actions conflict with the political interests of a supervisor or official.

2. Agency executives and politicians should protect the interests of public employees by aggressively seeking fair pay and working conditions and by shielding employees from direct or indirect political pressure.

3. Government should seek to recognize and reward outstanding employees in nonmonetary ways as well, including public rewards and incentives.

4. Officials with patronage power over employees outside the civil service system should treat the employees as if civil service protections applied and encourage ethical conduct regardless of political consequences.

5. Career public employees should abstain from public political activity such as campaigning or fund raising, although they should vote and be involved in civic or nonpartisan community roles.

6. A Model Code of Ethics for Public Employees:

a. *Duties Owed to Citizens*
—Every citizen with whom I deal should be treated with the same courtesy and respect that I would want if our roles were reversed.

—I will not treat citizens differently because of their race, national origin, religion, sex, age, or political beliefs.

—I will not engage in any action, such as a strike or slowdown, that endangers public health or safety. I will not engage in any such action unless all other attempts to resolve legitimate grievances about pay or working conditions have failed.

b. *Duties Owed to Taxpayers*
—I will work productively, efficiently, and honestly. I will look for ways to improve my own performance and that of my office because the goal of greater productivity is increased government services or lower taxes.

—I will not accept bribes or gifts, however small, that are given to me because of my public employment or with an intention to influence decisions made in my work.

—I will scrupulously avoid all conflicts of interest and will be sensitive to avoid even the appearance of impropriety.

c. *Duties Owed to Other Agencies and Public Employees*
—I will work closely with other agencies and their employees in an effort to help all of government be as productive as possible.

—I will share relevant information, ideas, and resources without being primarily concerned about interdepartmental politics.

d. *Duties Owed to Agency Executives and Politicians*
—I will treat my managers with the same respect and courtesy that I expect to receive as an employee.

—I will refuse to treat any customer more or less favorably than I would otherwise treat him or her to compromise my job performance in any way because doing so would advance the political interests of a supervisor or agency head.

—If I know of or reasonably suspect impropriety within government or my agency, including misconduct by my manager(s), I will notify the appropriate governmental authority so that the impropriety can be remedied. If reporting through channels would be futile or if the misconduct is ignored, I will contact the appropriate officials in other agencies or branches of government. Only if that does not result in a proper response to the impropriety will I inform the public or the media directly. All my actions in this regard will be thoughtful and responsible, rather than publicity seeking, but I will undertake them even though I may suffer personally as a result.

NOTES

1. *Rutan v. Republican Party of Ill.*, ____U.S. ____, 110 S.Ct. 2729, 111 L. Ed. 2d 52 (1990).
2. POLITICAL QUOTATIONS (D. Baker, ed. 1990).
3. Miller, *Rewards Encourage Workers to Blow the Whistle on Fraud*, L.A. Times, Aug. 6, 1991, at A5, col. 5.
4. CAL. GOV'T CODE 12650–12655 (1987).

5. *Strike Adds to Montana Snow Hazards as Plows Are Idle*, L.A. Times, Apr. 27, 1991, at A2, col. 1.

6. Interview with Theodore Kheel (by Art Athens, CBS), *reprinted in CCH* BUSINESS STRATEGIES 17, 389 (1990).

7. *Bush Makes Good on Veto Threat*, CONG. Q. 1874 (1990).

Lobbyists

No one seriously doubts the importance of the lobbying function. Georgia's 1877 constitution was unique when it declared lobbying to be a crime. A greater crime today would occur if government acted in the dark, unable to benefit from ethical lobbying. Representatives of particular industries, companies, or special interest groups supply information and perspective to legislators and other government officials that cannot be gained any other way. Especially when lobbyists representing differing interests compete, the resulting legislation or action ought to be a better product. Most lobbyists are honest, ethical people who view their profession as honorable. However, abuse by a few lobbyists of their special access to lawmakers or payment of bribes, great or small, has smeared the entire process.

Tennessee's experience is typical. About 350 lobbyists, three for each legislator, are registered with the Secretary of State's office. They represent both local and national businesses, as well as trade associations and groups such as the National Rifle Association. One legislator said,

This is not a full-time legislature. We don't have a full-time staff to research all the pieces of legislation that come through. We don't have any choice but to look at them for information. Most of them are here year after year, and you learn who you can trust to give you accurate information and who you can't.[1]

A Missouri legislator said, "I use lobbyists as much as they use me."[2]

In New York, there are more than 1,600 registered lobbyists. In Sacramento, California, legislators hear from nearly 800 lobbyists representing about 1,400 clients, double the number from ten years ago. In the first quarter of 1991, the top 100 lobbying firms brought in nearly $11 million. The growth in aggressive, organized lobbying at the state level prompted an Iowa House Speaker to say "We're witnessing the congressionalization of state legislatures."

Lobbyists work in five different roles. *The contact man* is the classic one-on-one purveyor of information and influence. In Washington, this role is less important because of the complexity of issues and the large, permanent congressional staffs. *The campaign organizer* creates grassroots support for a legislative program, organizing letter-writing campaigns or delegations of constituents to visit legislators. *The informant* may not be affiliated with a particular client but is a source of information and, in addition to using personal contacts, may testify publicly on legislative issues. *The watchdog* tracks the legislative calendar and the evolution of bills and alerts clients about developments affecting them. Finally, *the strategist* is a lobbyist's lobbyist who plans lobbying campaigns for others to execute. And lobbyists may fulfill one or more of these roles at the same time, while others specialize exclusively in one.

Even branches of government lobby each other. Judges seeking pay raises or judicial reform hire lobbyists to promote their cause. Every federal cabinet department has a congressional relations office, as do most noncabinet federal agencies. That represents a change from the Johnson administration's requirement that all executive branch lobbying be directed by the White House.

Lobbying of executive branch agencies is largely unregulated at both the federal and state levels. Recent HUD scandals amount to influence peddling by well-connected lobbyists. A member of the Republican National Committee made over $130,000 in consulting fees and was given equity in a Texas housing project valued at $4 million in exchange for his contacts with former HUD Secretary Pierce and his assistant, Deborah Gore Dean. He even wrote to them on Republican National Committee letterhead, rather than his own stationery. Congress may require disclosure of consultants and lobbyists who pursue federal funds in the executive branch and impose penalties if the recipients of federal grants, contracts, or loans used federal funds, directly or indirectly, to influence decision making.

The First Amendment protects lobbying. It is the right to "petition the Government for a redress of grievances." Efforts to limit lobbying that are aimed at huge corporate influence might also restrict citizen groups and individuals who want to communicate with public officials. Therefore, any proposed restriction should be studied carefully. In the language of constitutional law, the government must have a "compelling interest" in any regulation of the lobbying function and can only regulate if there is no "less restrictive alternative."

DISCLOSURE

An early federal effort to regulate lobbying by requiring disclosure was the Lobbying Act. In *U.S. v. Harriss*, a 1954 case holding that the act was constitutional, the Supreme Court said,

Present-day legislative complexities are such that individual members of Congress cannot be expected to explore the myriad pressures to which they are regularly subjected. Yet full realization of the American ideal of government by elected representatives depends to no small extent on their ability to properly evaluate such pressures. Otherwise the voice of the people may all too easily be drowned out by the voice of special interest groups seeking favored treatment while masquerading as proponents of the public weal. This is the evil which the Lobbying Act was designed to prevent.[3]

Most levels of government regulate lobbyists by requiring minimal disclosure of lobbyists' identity and clientele, together with reporting of major gifts to government officials. At least forty-six states have disclosure laws similar to the Lobbying Act, and all states require lobbyists to register. In addition, more than twenty states also regulate lobbying of executive branch officials.

Current disclosure laws do not disclose much. Of the eighty thousand people involved in lobbying activities in Washington, D.C., only about six thousand are registered as lobbyists because of the restrictive definition of *lobbyist* as one who spends a majority of his or her time personally asking legislators to support or oppose specific bills. Most lobbying is indirect or concerned with spreading information about a particular industry or trade association. The requirement that foreign agents register is diluted by the exception for lawyer-lobbyists representing foreign interests.

The typical law has ample loopholes and overlooks the frequent giving of small gifts. The prominent Tennessee liquor industry lobbyist has the generic lobbyists' nickname 'The Golden Goose." State legislators need never buy a meal while the legislature is in session. Especially in states where part-time legislators are away from home but unable to set up housekeeping, meals and entertainment are a welcome diversion. Special breakfast meetings, luncheons, receptions, and cocktail parties are continuously available. Other favors by lobbyists are less direct, but more valuable to the lawmaker. Two prominent Washington tax lobbyists helped Representative Beryl Anthony, an influential member of the tax-writing Ways and Means Committee, sell his interest in a hunting club to a third tax lobbyist.

While lobbyists are undeniably valuable as sources of information and ideas, there is no reason for legislators or other public officials to accept gifts of any kind, free meals, or equivalent benefits, whether disguised as receptions or fact-finding trips. Because of the need to avoid the appearance of impropriety, gifts or free meals should be refused even if they would be disclosed. An official who takes this admittedly extreme stand should have greater credibility with the voters.

It is appropriate for public officials to attend large social functions or seminars sponsored by industry or special interests when the lobbying component of the activity, if any, is indirect and diffused. And the public can benefit from officials' participation in such events when informal conversations or sharing of information expedites the public's business. However, the official who is paid $5,000, plus expenses, to speak for thirty minutes at a trade association meeting in Bermuda appears to have been bribed whether he knows it or not.

Lobbying disclosure laws should be extended and tightened. Every expenditure should be disclosed. Presumably such records are kept for reporting to the lobbyist's employer. Government officials should be required to make parallel filings of all gifts received or meals bought so disclosures can be cross-checked. Only if the disclosure requirements are comprehensive and enforced can the public know whether legislators are too close to corrupting influences. For example, if disclosure is required of gifts, including meals, of $50 or more, several lobbyists can jointly sponsor large gatherings (known in Tennessee as "choir practice") without triggering the disclosure requirements.

Even the strictest disclosure will not benefit the public unless the information is accessible. Because individuals are not likely to read the *Congressional Record* or examine the filings in a secretary of state's office, we rely on the media and citizen groups to serve as watchdogs, able to summarize and analyze the fruits of disclosure. Disclosure also enables public officials to know which interests a lobbyist really represents. Because a crooked lobbyist might not accurately disclose employers or expenditures, penalties for violating disclosure laws must be severe.

ACCESS

Good lobbyists are not primarily interested in a legislator's promise to vote a certain way on a certain bill. Rather, the lobbyist wants to build a long-term relationship of trust that results in access to the legislator. Access means that the public official will listen to arguments, read and rely on reports or statistics, and be willing to meet with lobbyists and their employers. Former Reagan aides Michael Deaver and Lyn Nofziger were flooded with lobbying clients, not because they could guarantee favorable executive branch decisions but because they had access to decision makers. Lobbyists who mislead legislators or put them in untenable positions will not be trusted or given access. A lobbyist who insists on every vote is unrealistic. The legislator's belief or the constituents' interests will differ from the lobbyist's from time to time.

Public officials should not provide greater access to a spokesperson for one viewpoint based on prior favors, gifts, or contributions. Access should be essentially equal for persons representing any interest that affects an official's public duties. It is common for lobbyist A, who needs the ear of a particular official, to hire lobbyist B to represent A's interest because B has a particularly close relationship with that official. In lobbying circles, it is known that certain legislators can only be approached through lobbyist B. Such relationships are like the famous mackerel that stinks and shines in the moonlight. They appear to be improper.

The official's former employees or associates should not have significantly greater access solely because of those relationships. Chapter 9 discusses the "revolving door," whereby former officials or public employees return to the political scene as lobbyists. California Representative Fortney Stark decried the abundance of former staffers descending on Congress to lobby for tax breaks: "It's obscene. They have just sold out for the big bucks to take on special-interest tax deductions on behalf of huge corporations and rich people."

It is natural for a former public official or staffer to have an advantage over over lobbyists because the basis for trust and confidence is already established. A legislator will naturally give more weight to the views of those who are already known and respected than to someone who is unknown. However, legislators should remain open to any opinion and should be willing to consider relevant information from any source. Even if they have no real advantage over other lobbyists, the appearance of impropriety justifies restraints on their activities.

An especially corrupt alliance between lawmakers and lobbyists occurs in the old, if rare, squeeze play. In concert with a lobbyist, one or more legislators introduce legislation threatening a certain industry or special interest group. The lobbyist then manages to be hired to lobby against the bill by claiming access to the sponsoring legislator. The bill then dies, and the lobbyist and the legislator(s) split the money.

CAMPAIGN CONTRIBUTIONS

While most officials have enough backbone that free meals and parties will not secure their vote, significant campaign contributions may be a different matter. An article appeared in 1960 entitled *How Payola Works in Politics*, by Assemblyman X, believed to have been the consummate

California politician, the late Jesse Unruh. He wrote that lobbyists, whom he called the Third House, frequently have more power than the two actual legislative houses combined. In one leadership fight, the lobbyists who had formerly shunned him now showed great concern for his problems.

"I understand you ran up a campaign deficit," one said. This was true. I still owed some $300. But before I could reply, the lobbyist went on:
"Don't give the *$2,000 deficit* another thought. Vote for Joe Green and we'll take care of it for you."
It wasn't until several other members of the Third House also offered to clean up my "$2,000 deficit" that I realized I was being offered a bribe.

The lobbyists' power to direct the substantial contributions of their clients is obvious. In addition to the ethical issues raised about campaign contributions in Chapter 2, lobbyist involvement in raising and distributing these funds presents special problems. Lobbyists are not particularly partisan. They must have access to members of both parties. Their role in the fund-raising process reflects a practical, apolitical approach.

Lobbyists also get hustled by politicians. In California, one lobbyist was invited to ninety different fund-raisers during one month, including fifteen on one night, with prices of $500 to $1,000 each. Buying tickets for all of them would have cost the special interests he represents $44,000. The lobbyist said, "It comes close to being blackmail or extortion. This is gold rush time. Those guys are trying to get as much money as they possibly can as fast as they can. The Legislature is in session, the lobbyists are all in town, and this is crunch time for major bills."[4]

Campaign contributions to Richard Nixon's reelection efforts have been described as the key event that led to an increase in milk price supports in 1971. They were the final step in an intense lobbying campaign. The day after a $35,000 first installment of a total of $255,000 in contributions, dairy industry representatives were invited to the White House. The president of the Mid-American Diarymen wrote to a member:

We diarymen as a body can be a dominant group. On March 23, 1971, along with nine other dairy farmers, I sat in the Cabinet Room of the White House across the table from the President of the United States, and heard him compliment the dairymen on their marvelous work in consolidating and unifying our industry and our involvement in politics. He said, "You people are my friends and I appreciate it."
Two days later an order came from the U.S. Department of Agriculture increasing the support price of milk . . . which added from $500 million to $700 million to dairy farmers' milk checks. We dairymen cannot afford to overlook this kind of economic benefit. Whether we like it or not, this is the way the system works.

Lobbyist-organized fund-raisers during a legislative session or well in advance of election campaigns are suspicious. The propriety of contributions directed by lobbyists can be measured in two ways: Is the contribution close in time to a vote or other action promoted by the lobbyist? Did the legislator make any explicit promises or implicit understandings that contributions would be rewarded? Public officials should refuse campaign contributions from lobbyists or the interests represented by lobbyists during legislative sessions when legislation is under consideration in which the contributor is especially interested. For example, there are always bills affecting banking or insurance companies, but there are identifiable times when critical matters affecting special interests are being discussed. Banking industry contributions at a time when usury limits are being debated are different in meaning than similar contributions at other times. If contributions are accepted at other times, the ground rules must be clear: the public official will not treat donors significantly more favorably than others, and the official's staff will be directed to restrain their behavior likewise.

ETHICAL GUIDELINES

1. Lobbyists should be viewed as one resource available to public officials for information and ideas about public business.

2. Public officials should not vote or take other action solely on the advice or request of lobbyists but should always apply independent judgment to their duties based on all available information, including that supplied by lobbyists.

3. Public officials should not accept meals, drinks, or gifts, however labeled, from lobbyists. Speaking fees or honoraria in excess of legitimate travel expenses should be refused. Large social or seminar functions may be attended because no undue influence on the official is likely to result.

4. Lobbyists should not receive access to a public official or the official's staff that competing lobbyists or any citizen would not also receive. Public officials should be especially cautious about dealings with lobbyists who are former employees or associates because of the appearance of impropriety. While it is natural to give preference to trusted sources of advice or information, officials should never appear to be heavily influenced by particular lobbyists.

5. Consistent with other ethical considerations about campaign financing, public officials should distance themselves from lobbyist-directed contributions and clearly communicate to contributors and their own staff that such contributions will not result in special access or considerations of the contributors' interests that are significantly different from access or consideration accorded to noncontributors.

6. Public officials should refuse campaign contributions from lobbyists

or their employers that are proffered near the time of a requested vote or action or during a time when the lobbyists' interests are receiving unusual legislative or governmental attention.

7. Public officials should support and implement stringent reporting and disclosure laws on both lobbyists and public officials so that the public can evaluate relationships between them. Such laws should have stiff penalties and sure enforcement mechanisms.

NOTES

1. Williams, *Lobbyists: Job of "Third House" is to Shape State's Laws*, Tennessean, Feb. 21, 1988, at B1, col. 1.

2. Hardy & Dohm, MISSOURI GOVERNMENT AND POLITICS 30 (1985) (quoted in Comment, *State Campaign Finance Law*, 55 MO. L. REV. 937, 948 note 50 (1990)).

3. 374 U.S. 612, 625, 74 S.Ct. 808, 816, 98 L.Ed. 989 (1954).

4. Gilliam, *It's "Gold Rush Time" in Capitol*, L.A. Times, Aug. 17, 1990, at A3, col. 5.

8

Paying Public Servants

Taxpayers and voters have ethical obligations, too. They have a duty to adequately compensate public servants with money, benefits, and appropriate working conditions. Legislators and executive officials have the duty to seek adequate funding for those purposes, even if such efforts are politically unpopular. Even if it is fair to hold legislative pay hostage to public dislike of budget deficits or tax rates, the pay for judges and agency executives should be boosted. Recent federal efforts to raise the pay of senior government executives and two hundred "critical" government workers, such as scientists, doctors, and researchers, were hindered because they were tied to congressional pay issues.

The problem is just as great for less visible jobs. If a federal judge threatens to resign because of insultingly low pay, that's news. We're less likely to hear about the teacher who reluctantly resigns to make more money in another job.

The 1989 controversy over federal pay raises occurred despite the Federal Pay Comparability Act of 1970, which was designed to remove politics from federal pay decisions. However, the increases recommended under that law have seemed so high that Congress has always approved lower pay hikes or none at all. Tactically, public employee raises ought to come in small, automatic increments, rather than a major, sudden pay hike.

As discussed earlier, money is not the primary motivation for those in elected or appointed positions, nor for career civil servants. Other satisfactions flow from public life or the relative security of a civil service job. In deciding how much to pay for those services, it is fair to consider the nonmonetary advantages of public service. In addition, public employees want to be treated with respect, not referred to in politicians' speeches as "pointy-headed bureaucrats" or other epithets that constitute image bashing.

A substantial raise in congressional pay will not cause people to run for office who would not otherwise do so, nor will it cause incumbents to run for reelection who would otherwise retire. (Two-thirds of the richest U.S. senators and one-half of the richest representatives, all multi-millionaires, voted against recent efforts to raise legislative pay.) However, it will minimize financial pressures on public servants that lead to ethical misconduct or the appearance of impropriety. Former Arkansas State Attorney General Steve Clark was convicted of falsifying expense accounts and travel vouchers, apparently to supplement his income. While that conduct is not excusable, consider that his pay was only $25,000 per year.

FAIR PAY

The average pay gap between the private and public sectors is estimated at 24 percent. University of Chicago economist Gary Becker argues that the pay disparities are at the highest levels of government. The difference between private and public pay for positions such as senior attorneys, accountants, scientists, or engineers is greater than for lower-level or clerical jobs. A government lawyer with responsibilities similar to those of a corporate attorney makes $64,026, compared to about $110,000 in the private sector, a pay gap of 62 percent.[1] Furthermore, there are regional disparities. Federal pay for a manager in Tulsa may be comparable to private sector managers but is woefully inadequate in New York City.

We cannot afford to lose good public employees to private industry or discourage them from entering government service. The costs of training replacement workers, who may themselves leave shortly, is obvious. The most effective public servants are the ones most likely to be recruited by industry, leaving a work force that is less skilled. And it is possible that the very employees lost because of low pay and inadequate recognition are also the most ethical. Rather than working less for low pay or supplementing their income improperly, they reluctantly move to the private sector in order to achieve adequate support for themselves and their families.

Co-author Michael Cody recently experienced that frustration following four years as Tennessee's Attorney General. After exhausting his savings while in government service in order to maintain a modest life-style and put his children through college, he resigned to reenter law practice. He refused to borrow money and further weaken his finances in order to continue in the job—to do so would have also exposed him to temptations that he could have resisted but did not need to face. Nobody made him take that job. He enjoyed the work all four years and did not borrow any money. It was his choice to make a financial sacrifice to take a public service job. He felt he could afford to give four years to public service.

The chairman of IBM and the governor of California both run enterprises with annual revenues in excess of $50 billion and supervise hundreds of thousands of employees. Yet the businessman's base salary is ten times the governor's, and the businessman gets bonuses. The mayor of Little Rock, Arkansas, is paid nothing. Legislators in Rhode Island receive $5 per day that the legislature is in session.[2]

While no one expects government jobs to pay as well as private business, there should be greater correlation farther down the career ladder. Clerk-typists and similar clerical positions should be paid nearly the same as the private sector to minimize turnover. Agency executives are more likely to be attracted by the chance to serve in government and will be more satisfied with disparate pay scales. Elected officials or high-level appointees are willing to sacrifice financially for a short time in order to serve the public. In order to keep effective officials longer, the sacrifices of public service must be minimized.

PERKS

If this section were titled "John Sununu Gets His Wings," it would quickly become an obscure, dated reference because the abuse of perks (perquisites of office) will continue and new examples come to light. As the poet Edna St. Vincent–Millay said, "It is not true that life is one damn thing after another. It's one damn thing over and over." Sununu, President Bush's first Chief of Staff, was the subject of outrage when it was learned that he used government jets for purely personal trips, as well as trips with mixed governmental and political or personal objectives. He paid the commercial fare, plus $1, for trips that cost the government $4,000 per hour so that he could visit his Boston dentist, attend a football game, and go skiing.[3] The White House quickly conceded that those trips abused the policy and began to monitor them more closely. In the wake of Sununu's troubles, a report that Vice President Quayle used an Air Force jet for a golfing trip received little public attention. Security concerns mean that neither the President nor the Vice President should fly commercial. The President's entourage and accompanying press contingent would fill an entire airliner, anyway. However, other officials, such as Cabinet officials, should not use military aircraft costing thousands of dollars an hour only to reimburse the government the cost of a regular ticket, a few hundred dollars.

Even legislators want this perk. The best case could be made for House Speaker Thomas Foley, who is third in line for presidential succession. An attempt to pass legislation giving him full-time access to a $19-million military jet was abandoned after it received adverse publicity.[4]

In any job, the perks of a company car or free samples are sometimes more fun than the salary. People brag about their perks. When good public servants make a tremendous financial sacrifice in their government job, it seems almost mean to begrudge them a few perks. But, as Sununu showed, perks can be abused. Former Education Secretary Lauro F. Cavazos did fly commercial but may have given his frequent-flier bonus points to his wife. They were government property. A greater impropriety may be when government officials fly on corporate aircraft when those corporations do business with their agencies.

OUTSIDE INCOME

> The rule, then, for a public man, or one who feels a calling to become such, in a free country in modern times, seems to me this: Keep yourself independent, which includes first, as a matter of course, a total discarding of that silly and little-minded desire to rival your rich neighbor in his way of living, and secondly, that you should be possessed of the means of maintaining yourself, be this by the possession of a moderate property or a profession or trade; and, that these means may be easily acquired (for otherwise you would not feel independent), reduce your wants to the lowest degree compatible with a continued communion with your fellow-beings, on the one hand, and a decorous but modest maintenance of your family and the sound education of your children, on the other.
>
> —Francis Lieber, *Manual of Politics* (1838)

Although public employees at lower levels may hold part-time jobs without raising ethical concerns so long as their full-time job performance does not suffer, outside income received by more prominent public officials is troubling. Early in American history, Daniel Webster insisted that his "retainer be refreshed" before he would run for reelection and continue to protect New England mercantile interests.[5] Today, that would be called a bribe, unless it came in the form of an honorarium.

The dangers of honoraria were discussed in Chapter 4. Honoraria are paid to legislative staff members, as well as legislators, for example, $2,000 for a lunchtime speech. Aides can make thousands of dollars per day by bunching such appearances. In 1985 and 1986, when tax reform was taking shape, the staff director of the Senate Finance Committee received nearly $38,000 for speeches and turned down much more. Such payments to staffers are obvious efforts to obtain unfair access to influence decision making.

In addition to gifts and honoraria that should be refused, public officials may have steady income from a profession or investments that affects their independent judgment. In 1977, Congress imposed limits on outside earned income but did not limit unearned income from investments or family trusts. There are two distinctions between earned and unearned income for the purposes of ethics. First, the earned income represents time away from the duties of the public officer. When the office is deemed to be a full-time job, the official's full attention should be given to it. Second, the outside income is from an employer or several clients who could fire the official if they dislike a vote or other action taken in the public job. A lawyer-legislator who receives a retainer or steady business from a bank would avoid displeasing the bank in legislative matters, lest the legal business be taken elsewhere. That threat is an influence on the official that has the appearance of impropriety.

Federal law now prohibits government employees from earning any money from outside activity involving writing, speaking, or personal appearances. Government employees who moonlighted as preachers or sports writers were covered, as well as legislative staffers reaping unearned honoraria.

The President's Commission on Federal Ethics Law Reform recommended that senior employees in all three branches of government be restricted by a uniform percentage cap on outside earned income, although the President could exempt categories of earned income from the cap that do not present significant issues of ethical propriety or interfere with the full performance of job duties. The commission found:

In order for an employee to do his job properly, however, such activities need to be restricted in time and scope to avoid the real risk that outside income-producing activities will take time and energy away from official activities (even if only through the accumulation of such minor intrusions such [sic] as occasional phone calls and concomitant use of support staff to take phone messages) . . . paid outside work is more likely to engross the federal employee to the extent of creating an interference with the individual's basic duties. This seems particularly likely to occur when the outside income assumes a substantial proportion of an official's compensation in relation to the federal salary.[6]

In theory, income received from investments takes little time and will continue regardless of the official's public duties. But an official can spend too much time managing investments. A judge who runs a large-scale rental empire from chambers may face no conflicts of interest, except the most basic one—not giving taxpayers their money's worth. Or the investments themselves can be conflicts of interest.

For full-time officials, the choice is clear. If you cannot survive without potentially conflicting outside income, do not take the job. Even if the income is earned from real work that does not present a conflict, the official should be devoting the workday to the public's work. Time devoted to managing investments or a personal business should be treated no differently. In 1986, only 11 percent of state legislators held full-time legislative positions, but the trend is toward full-time state legislatures in about two-thirds of the states. In California, about one-third of state lawmakers hold no other job. Evaluating the conflict caused by outside income to a full-time legislator is easier than for part-timers, but we lose an element of participatory democracy when we lose part-time legislators who must work in the real world to support themselves.

Another form of outside work is service on boards of directors of either for-profit or nonprofit corporations. White House Counsel C. Boyden Gray, charged with directing Bush administration ethics, resigned as chairman of the board of his family-owned communications company. He received several hundred thousand dollars from that position while serving as counsel to Vice President Bush, although he only spent four to six days per year on company matters. The President's commission recommended that service by senior federal employees of all branches on for-profit boards be prohibited and that service on nonprofit boards be reviewed on a case-by-case basis. With regard to for-profit boards of directors, the commission found:

Such board memberships not only can take away time and distract an employee's attention away from his official duties, but can risk the abuse of public office for private gain, by creating an appearance that there has been an official endorsement of private profit-making activities. . . . Compensated board memberships also create the potential for evasion of the limitation [on honoraria]. Companies that previously would have paid an official for a public speech might instead pay substantial directors' fees.[7]

Part-time officials are expected to retain their full-time jobs, so long as they can adapt and meet their public responsibilities. The major problem then is avoiding conflicts of interest. The county commissioner who sells insurance for a living obviously should not sell insurance to the county, but he also should not use his influence as a commissioner to sell insurance to county vendors or employees. When the part-time public official is a full-time lawyer, it is difficult to know when beginning to represent a client whether a conflict of interest will develop. Therefore, the lawyer–public official should make it a condition of employment, agreed to by the client, that if a conflict occurs between the client's interests and the duty of the attorney to be an independent, ethical public official, the client will have to hire a new lawyer.

The 1991 confirmation hearings on Lamar Alexander's nomination to be Secretary of Education revealed an exceptionally bright, effective public servant with the Midas touch. While Governor of Tennessee, he consolidated three separate loans totaling $132,000 into one unsecured loan at the prime interest rate. While Governor, he was one of seven men who spent time helping find a buyer for a Knoxville newspaper. He received $620,000 on an investment of no money. While he was Governor, his wife invested $8,900 in the stock of a for-profit corrections company. When it began doing business with the state, she swapped her stock for shares in an insurance company that she sold for $142,000 five years later.[8]

No one can seriously argue that the Governor or his wife acted unethically, but his desire to make money while in a powerful government position created an unfortunate appearance. Even the senators who were concerned about the appearance voted to confirm Secretary Alexander, except for Senator Tom Harkins, who said, "I somehow think we have the wrong nominee here. We need him as Secretary of the Treasury."[9]

There is little regulation of outside income at the state level. For example, California Assembly Speaker Willie Brown mixes business and his law practice with his public duties. A client who hires Brown knows not only that Brown is extremely talented and well respected but also that his dual role as Speaker will get the attention of anyone with whom he deals. A former Acting State Treasurer claims that Brown pressured her to send state business to one of his clients. Speaker Brown denies any impropriety.[10] But mixing business and government roles will always create the appearance of impropriety.

Idaho Senator Steven Symms, a part-owner of a winery, tried to convince his colleagues on the Finance Committee to reduce a tax on wineries. He denied having a conflict of interest, arguing that it was a "parallel interest": "Just because I happen to know something about it doesn't mean it's a conflict."[11] But it does mean that it appears to be a conflict.

Public officials should disclose all outside sources of income in detail so that the public can be informed about potential or actual conflicts of interest. If client confidentiality would be infringed by naming names, the income should at least be grouped in fairly specific categories: banks, insurance companies, and so on. Unearned income should also be reported in detail without masking the actual sources of dividends or other monies. If it comes from First National Bank stock, the public deserves to know that.

DISCLOSURE

At a minimum, public officials should disclose complete financial details and all associations with business or other interests that might result in conflicts of interest. Public officials resent disclosure requirements because such requirements seem to imply distrust or because they have less privacy about financial matters than other citizens. Two members of the Los Angeles city commissions resigned, rather than make the financial disclosures required by a new ethics law. The law requires the officials to report the precise value of investments, all real estate holdings, and loans and list income earned by their spouses and dependent children, as well as listing the names of stockbrokers, business associates, and partners. One of the resignees said, "The intrusions to our private lives were so great, I could not continue. They go well beyond what should be necessary to ensure a person doing his job honestly and properly."[12] Those objections do not outweigh the need to avoid both impropriety and the appearance of impropriety. Full disclosure is at least a step in that direction.

Full financial disclosure is a justified imposition on public officials. In the New Testament story of the rich, young ruler, the test of his commitment was whether he was willing to sell all that he had and give it to the poor. While public officials should not impoverish themselves, full financial disclosure is a fair test of their commitment. The importance of public office means that the public should be able to judge for itself whether the official is laboring under a conflict of interest, even though the official may disagree. The public cannot make that judgment unless there is full disclosure.

Current disclosure requirements are weak. Federal financial disclosure consists of broad categories. *Forbes* magazine used the example of the late Pennsylvania Senator John Heinz who accurately filled out the federal form by listing an asset, H. J. Heinz stock, and checking the valuation box marked "$250,000 and above." The stock was worth $363 million.[13] Elected and appointed federal officials covered by the law do not have to declare the value or existence of personal residences, no matter how many or how grand, unless they generate income. The theory behind simple categories of assets or income is sound. There is evidence of a potential conflict of interest whether a public official owns one share of IBM stock or one million. However, judging an individual public official's susceptibility to influence by the conflict of interest requires an accurate picture of the official's net worth.

The disclosure required of public officials in Georgia is somewhat more stringent. Their annual financial disclosure statements must list:

1. honoraria or speaking fees related to the public office of more than $101;
2. all fiduciary and business positions held by the official, including the title of the position, the name and address of the business and its principal activity;
3. all involvement in businesses in which the official's ownership interest was at least 10 percent or which was worth more than $20,000;
4. each parcel of real estate worth more than a net figure after subtracting indebtedness of more than $20,000; and
5. all annual payments of more than $20,000 from the state or any state agency to any of the businesses in which the official has an ownership interest.[14]

Regardless of whether relevant law requires less to be disclosed, public officials should publicly report:

—complete tax returns for themselves and spouse;

—financial statements showing net worth, amounts, and sources of income, major expenditures, and all assets owned, both real property and other investments, including identifying all co-owners;

—all nongovernmental positions held, whether paid or unpaid;

—involvement in any pending litigation and all litigation or bankruptcy within the past five years; and

—all gifts, travel, entertainment, meals given to them while in office.

Complete disclosure is a paperwork headache, especially the first time. New York's disclosure requirements may go too far, requiring that all government employees earning more than $30,000 (roughly 70,000) file a detailed seven-page form. The resulting 490,000-page blizzard would hamper enforcement of ethics laws against the much smaller number of key employees who are likely to have major conflicts of interest.

Complete disclosure may keep qualified, sincere people from seeking public office who are unwilling to invade the privacy of family or associates. That is unfortunate, but in view of the harm to be avoided, acceptable. Disclosure should take place at least annually, with more frequent updates required when there are significant changes in any item.

Full disclosure may reveal improprieties that campaign finance reporting would miss. For example, former House Speaker Jim Wright earned $55,000 in royalties from a 117-page book of speech excerpts and anecdotes. The story gradually leaked out that he received a 55 percent royalty and that a House staffer worked on the book on government time. Although there is a limit on honoraria he could receive, there was no limit on this outside income. One of his developer friends, who bought $6,000 worth of books, said, "I was just trying to make a contribution to Jim's income. I couldn't give him any money. There are rules against that. So I bought his book."[15] If disclosure had been required, the impropriety might never have been committed.

BLIND TRUSTS

If disclosure reveals that a public official has personal holdings that create conflicts of interest, a blind trust is commonly suggested to resolve the impropriety. Secretary of State James Baker owned a large amount of bank stock while he was Treasury Secretary in the Reagan administration. He could not have recused himself from all official decisions that might have affected his banking interests. That would have left him only with decisions about what to serve in the employee cafeteria. And a blind trust that required the trustee to keep the bank stocks would have been futile. Secretary Baker would still have known that his net worth was tied to the banking industry.

At the same time, requiring Secretary Baker or his trustee to sell the bank stocks and invest in other industries would have triggered substantial capital gains taxes. Dedicated public officials should not have to pay a tax to serve in government.

The tax laws provide that any public official who is ethically required to sell certain holdings be permitted a tax-free rollover into a neutral investment, such as a diversified mutual fund, so that the ethical choice does not cost money. The taxable gain is not recognized until the neutral investment vehicle was sold after government service or the particular conflict ended. The President's Commission on Federal Ethics Law Reform recommended this change in the tax laws based upon a study that showed that "some of the best qualified candidates for high level policymaking positions decline Presidential appointments because of the tax consequences flowing from the need to sell their investment assets to eliminate conflicts."[16] The commission recommended that an agency head or comparable authority certify the need for divestiture so that the tax break would not be abused.

Not all blind trusts are blind; some peek a lot. If a governor owns a farm, a chain of shopping centers, and a car rental franchise and is unwilling to liquidate those assets, a blind trust does not minimize the conflict of interest. He wants to make sure those assets are managed well while he is in office, and he intends to take direct control of them again when he leaves office. Meanwhile, the governor's actions affecting farmers, shopping center developers, and the car rental business are suspect, even though the governor is a person of high integrity.

President Reagan's assets, other than his California ranch, were in stocks and bonds to which he had no special attachment. He willingly consented to a truly blind trust. The trustee had the power to buy and sell without the President's knowledge or consent. The President's tax returns showed the amount of taxable income from the trust, but not its sources. While the President might take action to benefit business or the stock market generally, he could not benefit particular companies or industries knowing he would thereby gain financially.

Public officials whose investments create potential conflicts of interest should place those assets in a blind trust and give the trustee as much power as possible over the disposition or reinvestment of the assets. If conditions are placed on the trustee's powers, such as forbidding them to dispose of certain assets, those conditions should be publicly disclosed. When the creation of a blind trust is justified, regardless of conditions placed on the trustee, the public official should not be involved in the management of trust assets.

GIFTS

In 1988, the Recruit scandal in Japanese politics gave us a refreshing sense that the United States is at least ahead of Japan in the field of political ethics. Not only are everyday gifts to Japanese politicians much more frequent and expensive, but the huge gifts of stock to high Japanese officials by the company Recruit Cosmos highlighted the much wider acceptance of the practice. Japanese candidates routinely buy votes by giving money for weddings or funerals. The *Wall Street Journal* quoted one Japanese professor's Japanese "Rules of Morality": "If it doesn't come out, it is OK. If it comes out, blame it on an aide. If that doesn't work, say everyone does it. That always works."[17]

Somehow those "Rules of Morality" sound familiar. The difference between Japan and the United States on the question of gifts to public officials is only a matter of degree. Gifts to members of Congress must only be reported if they are worth more than $250. But since they can accept gifts valued at more than $250 only from family members, there will be no such reporting.[18] Virtually all gifts to public officials are from businesses or individuals who expect to gain an advantage as a result. The impropriety is the same whether the gift is baseball tickets or a new car, although one is more visible than the other. For the same reason, the once-frequent congressional practice of taking free rides on corporate aircraft has become infrequent. How could any such ride be worth less than $250?

Public officials should refuse all gifts from persons or groups who wish to influence the official. Public officials should also refuse gifts from employees under their supervision, except for officewide gifts for special occasions or other gifts of nominal value. The Los Angeles City Ethics Commission ruled that city employees could accept a free cup of coffee and a doughnut ("common refreshments") from persons doing business with the city. Free parking validations while on city business are also acceptable.[19]

Some states permit legislators to accept up to $50 (or more) of food or drink per meal from lobbyists without disclosure by either the lobbyists or the legislator. They can accept any number of $49 meals from a lobbyist without disclosure required of either the lobbyist or legislator. The limitation may be interpreted so that, for example, four lobbyists together could spend $196 for one legislator's meal. By equally dividing the tab, the lobbyists could obliterate public knowledge of the event.

One state legislator, accustomed to lobbyists' free meals, called his favorite lobbyist and said, "Tonight is my wedding anniversary, and I want to take my wife somewhere nice." The lobbyist replied, "I'm sorry. I have to be out of town tonight." "That's all right, I don't need you. Just loan me your credit card." When the legislature is in session in most states, no legislator need ever personally buy a meal or a drink. Even if they are so inured to the system that freebies do not influence them, the appearance of impropriety demands that the practice end. The business lunch is a noble American institution. However, when it is held at a four-star restaurant, instead of the legislative cafeteria, suspicion rises.

The Office of Government Ethics forbids executive branch employees from accepting anything of value from anyone who "has interests which may be substantially affected" by the employees' official activities, including news media. However, Congress prohibits acceptance of gifts aggregating over $100 from a person with a direct interest in legislation before Congress but has no limitation on the acceptance of meals and entertainment. The President's commission recommended the adoption of uniform gift rules for all branches of government.

If the official does not receive a bill, is it a gift or a loan or something else? Senator Alfonse D'Amato did not disclose as a liability legal fees he owed his attorney for representing him during a two-year ethics investigation. Those fees undoubtedly total thousands and thousands of dollars, but the Senator was not billed for at least two years.

The nation's top 12,000 officials, primarily presidential appointees, must file annual financial disclosure statements publicly.[20] About 200,000 middle-management employees must file them confidentially with their agencies or departments.

Officials should do their best to ensure that close friends or relatives do not accept gifts from persons or companies affected by the officials' public duties. There is the same potential for improper influence whether the gift goes directly to the official or to people with whom the official has a close relationship. Even if there is not actual influence, the improper appearance of such a gift should be avoided. The current ethics regulations enforced by the federal Office of Personnel Management states: "The interest of a spouse, minor, child, or other member of an employee's immediate household is considered to be an interest of the employee."[21] Limiting improper gifts to household members is insufficient. Gifts or favors to other relatives or friends should be forbidden if the effect on the official is equally possible. If the official is unable to keep the friend or relative from accepting the gift, he or she should promptly disclose it in order to avoid the appearance of impropriety. The possibility of disclosure may deter influence seekers from offering such gifts.

Gifts by civic organizations or groups like the Girl Scouts are more likely to be motivated by a desire for publicity or recognition. There is no impropriety in accepting traditional gifts such as a beautiful piece of handicraft under those circumstances. When appropriate, gifts of food or clothing should be passed on to be distributed to the less fortunate.

Ceremonial gifts between heads of government or agencies fall into the same category. As a matter of etiquette, the Governor of Idaho will hand out cases of Idaho potatoes on official trips. Visiting mayors distribute products of local pride. The President receives gifts, often outrageously expensive, from foreign heads of state. Like the President, all public officials who receive gifts in the course of their official duties should report them and treat them as public property. If the gifts are elaborate or expensive, they might be displayed in a museum or discreetly sold for the benefit of the public treasury. Even if the ceremonial gift is intended to influence the official, that will not occur if the official treats the gift as government property.

ETHICAL GUIDELINES

1. The public owes a duty to public employees at all levels of government to provide adequate pay, benefits, and working conditions. Elected officials and agency officials should work effectively with the public and the legislatures to ensure that public employees are fairly compensated, even if fair pay is not politically popular.

2. Full-time officials should not receive income from outside activities, other than passive income from investments or businesses in which they have an ownership interest but do not actively manage.

3. Full-time public officials should not serve on the board of directors of a for-profit corporation or receive pay for serving on the board of a nonprofit corporation. Unpaid service on a nonprofit corporation's board should be limited so that there is no interference with the officials' public duties.

4. Part-time public officials who are expected to maintain other full-time employment must avoid all conflicts of interest, as well as the appearance of conflicts, between the full-time job and their public duties.

5. All public officials should fully disclose all sources and amounts of outside income, although the names of professional clients may be replaced with specific client categories if disclosure would violate confidentiality.

6. Public officials who own investments or businesses that pose conflicts of interest should sell those assets. If it is impractical or unfair to require divestiture, those assets should be placed in a blind trust over which the trustee has complete control, with minimal reporting to the official. If the official insists on placing conditions on the trustee's power, such conditions should be made public, but in no event should the official continue to actively manage the asset. No blind trust is required if the

holdings are so small that disclosure by itself will minimize the appearance of impropriety.

7. Public officials should refuse all speaking fees or honoraria from companies or industries that might be seeking influence over them, although officials may accept reimbursement for travel expenses if such reimbursement is publicly disclosed.

8. Public officials should refuse all gifts, however characterized, except for gifts from civic groups that seek no influence on the official and ceremonial gifts between government officials. Any gift accepted by an official is public property and should be reported and turned over to the government.

9. Public officials should attempt to keep close friends or relatives of the official from accepting gifts or favors from persons or companies affected by the officials' public duties. If the elected official cannot prevent the acceptance of a gift or favor that has the appearance of impropriety, the official should promptly disclose that such a gift was made in order to dispel the improper appearance.

10. Elected officials should make complete disclosure of all financial, business, and personal dealings so that the public can evaluate whether the official is influenced by a conflict of interest. The disclosure should be wide-ranging and almost certainly more than may be required by law.

NOTES

1. *Beltway Brain Drain: Why Civil Servants Are Making Tracks*, Bus. Wk., Jan. 23, 1989, at 60, 61.

2. Witt, *Are Our Governments Paying What It Takes to Keep the Best and the Brightest?*, Governing, Dec. 1988, at 30, 36.

3. *Sununu Travel Policy Violations Cited in Report*, L.A. Times, Apr. 26, 1991, at A1, col. 1.

4. Fritz, *Winging It with Free Air Travel*, L.A. Times, Apr. 26, 1991, at A, col. 1.

5. Weld, *Public Corruption Is Costing Us Too Much*, Wash. Post, May 2–8, 1988, at 22, 23 (nat'l wkly. ed.).

6. TO SERVE WITH HONOR: REPORT OF THE PRESIDENT'S COMMISSION ON FEDERAL ETHICS LAW REFORM, Mar. 1989, at 37.

7. *Id.* at 40.

8. Pound & Stout, *Bush Nominee Alexander's Investment Successes Have Made Senate Investigators Very Inquisitive*, Wall St. J., Mar. 5, 1991, at A16, col. 1.

9. Jackson, *Panel Backs Alexander as Education Secretary*, L.A. Times, Mar. 14, 1991, at A4, col. 1.

10. Morain & Jacobs, *World of Politics, Law Often Mix for Speaker*, L.A. Times, Apr. 1. 1991, at A1, col. 3.

11. Birnbaum, *Idaho Senator Fails to Keep Tax Bite from Hitting Home*, Wall St. J., Oct. 18, 1990, at A8, col. 5.

12. Fritsch & Mitchell, *Two Members Quit Police Board over Ethics Law*, L.A. Times, Mar. 5, 1991, at B1, col. 5.

13. Jereski, *How Not to Value a Politician*, Forbes, Oct. 26, 1987, at 352.

14. GA. CODE ANN. 21–5–50 (1988).

15. Herbers, *Demand for Ethics in Government Has Outstripped Supply*, N.Y. Times, June 19, 1988, at 4, col. 1.

16. TO SERVE WITH HONOR: REPORT OF THE PRESIDENT'S COMMISSION ON FEDERAL ETHICS LAW REFORM, Mar. 1989, at 26.

17. Darlin, *New Scandal Obsesses but Hardly Surprises the Cynical Japanese*, Wall St. J., Dec. 27, 1988, at 1, col. 6.

18. *House Approves $23,200 Increase in Senate Pay*, L.A. Times, July 31, 1991, at A3, col. 6.

19. Murphy, *Free Coffee No Longer Brews Up Controversy for Public Employees*, L.A. Times, May 18, 1991, at B3, col. 5.

20. Ethics in Government Act of 1978, Pub. L. No. 95–201, 201–205, 92 Stat. 1824 (1978).,

21. 5 C.F.R. 734–735, 737.

9

The Revolving Door

One of the great traditions in American public life has been the willingness of men and women to leave private jobs temporarily and join government service. We do not want a government composed only of civil servants. The generous work of non–career employees reflects our basic democratic view of government. At the federal level, there are about six thousand political jobs in which turnover occurs near the beginning of a new administration and continues while it is in office. Turnover does create recruitment problems and the loss of valuable experience. At the Justice Department, the annual turnover rate is 14 percent.

The recent disclosures about corruption in the Defense Department procurement process highlight one critical element in all government contracting and lobbying—the use of former agency employees to represent industry. There is an inherent conflict of interest in the "revolving door" between government and the private sector. Government employees may think the chances of being hired by industry will be enhanced if they decide matters in a certain way or are more cooperative generally. Furthermore, recent agency employees may have an unfair advantage over private competitors because of their knowledge or access. Because it is impractical (and probably unconstitutional) to prohibit former agency employees from working in companies affected by that agency, there should be clear guidelines that remove most actual conflicts of interest, as well as the public perception of those conflicts.

In 1988, Archibald Cox's testimony before a subcommittee of the Senate Governmental Affairs Committee identified four problems with the revolving door:

1. The official, while still in office but thinking of work as a lobbyist, will be tempted to curry favor with prospective employers or clients.
2. The ex-official will find it all too easy to use inside information not available to others for the benefit of his private employer or client.
3. The ex-official will often be able to trade upon the habits of deferring to his advice and wishes engendered during the days when he was senior to, or at least a more influential official than, those with whom he now deals in a different capacity.
4. At best, the insidious influences described by Senator Paul Douglas come into play. The ex-official lobbyist comes as a friend, an insider, "player" or "actor" in the current jargon. At a minimum, he gets a different hearing or preferred access. That advantage alone may make the difference. No party to litigation or lawyer would be willing to have the judge hear only the evidence and argument of the other side, still less to have them heard alone in chambers. And with the hearing, the risk of the influence of friendship, common political interests, and reciprocal backscratching grow.[1]

The activities of former Presidents relate to the revolving door, even when they do not present typical conflicts of interest. Obviously, their earning power as authors, speakers, or board members is enhanced by their experience. President Reagan's fee of $2 million for one week's visit to Japan might be fair but for the taxpayers' expense in providing Secret Service protection for him while there. And there are direct conflicts of interest when such ventures are discussed while the President is still in office, as happened in that case. While reasonable people see no problem with ex-Presidents making up for money lost while in public service, the better examples are President Ford and Carter, who combine money-earning activities with charitable and humanitarian efforts.

THE VALUE OF THE REVOLVING DOOR

Movement between parallel jobs in government and the private sector should not be prohibited, even if that were possible. The revolving door is a natural phenomenon because the best source of talent for industry is the pool of current or recent employees of the agency or department that regulates or supports that industry. And the nature of civil service pay, advancement, and working conditions makes the jump from government employment understandable. At the same time, industry executives may seek a governmental job both because of genuine public service motives and the invaluable lessons about how the agency really works.

There are distinct advantages to the efficient operation of government when experienced, high-level executives spend a reasonable amount of time in a government job. Those executives have been trained to operate in a profit-centered environment and are less patient with delays, red tape, and waste. Even the best career bureaucrats may become inured to inefficient tendencies in government. The government normally gets the benefit of well-informed, decisive leadership for below-market rates. Their practical experience is valuable to the agency, which might not otherwise have the benefit of recent, firsthand knowledge about the industry with which it is concerned. Finally, exposure to the agency makes the employees even more marketable if they wish to return to private business. Frequently, people who spent a few years early in their career working at lower levels in an agency return after they have risen within industry and are even better equipped to perform governmental duties.

At the same time, agencies benefit from the service of lower-level employees who plan to leave after learning all they can from the governmental perspective. They might be able to make more money or build security faster by beginning a private job sooner, but they are willing to work for less in exchange for the experience. For example, young lawyers interested in taxation, securities, or other specialized, heavily regulated fields gain the equivalent of postgraduate study by working for the Internal Revenue Service (IRS), the National Labor Relations Board (NLRB), the Securities Exchange Commission (SEC), and so on. One graduate of the revolving door said, "The experience is costly, but also priceless."[2]

However, the potential for unethical and dishonest conduct is so great that special rules are justified to regulate the revolving door. Even though the vast majority of people who move between the public and private sectors do nothing improper, there is at least an appearance of impropriety that must be addressed. In 1982, Thomas Vartanian was the chief lawyer for the Federal Home Loan Bank Board and helped write the new rules that freed savings and loan institutions from many regulatory constraints. In 1988, he billed $12 million for his work in S&L mergers and acquisitions, the result of S&L failures in a deregulated environment. He said, "People don't come out of a regulatory agency in Washington and become a plumber." While Vartanian's conduct is legal and he obviously did not foresee the S&L failures that have occurred, the hindsight is ironic.[3]

As with other aspects of public service ethics, appearances are as important as reality. The danger is that employers may think they are buying greater access when someone is hired fresh from government service or that clients or customers will choose an attorney or lobbyist based on a perception that the recency or importance of the former government job gives him or her an advantage. The other possibility is that the former official will make those claims, either directly or indirectly. The former official who picks up the phone in the client's presence and whose call is answered immediately by a current official may not be told anything confidential, but the client has an impression of real power. It is natural that a former official's call will be answered, but the former official must make it clear that he or she expects no information or action to which others are not entitled.

Lawyers who have been through the revolving door have a specific ethical restraint imposed by both current codes of legal ethics. Rule 8.4(e) of the *Model Rules of Professional Conduct* states: "It is professional misconduct for a lawyer to state or imply an ability to influence improperly a government agency or official." Over fifty years ago, the ethics committee of the American Bar Association declared that "statements of the lawyer's experience in and acquaintance with the various departments and agencies of the government . . . is not only bad taste but ethically improper."

In a sliding door arrangement, the California Insurance Commissioner hired two former state lawyers with expertise in state insurance matters at $196 an hour to prepare insurance rate-setting regulations, represent the department in court, and talk to reporters. (The State Attorney General's office would provide lawyers at a cost of $75 an hour.) The two lawyers are not representing private interests before state government but are assisting the government itself as outside consultants.

THE FEDERAL ETHICS IN GOVERNMENT ACT OF 1978

A starting point for ethical rules about the revolving door is the federal law that address it. The Ethics in Government Act deals with financial disclosure by government officials and the appointment of special prosecutors to pursue alleged misconduct by certain executive branch officials. It also sets limits on private business activities by former government employees.[4] Current law does not require that former employees receive compensation for lobbying or other work before the agency which employed them in order to be criminally liable. The President's Commission on Federal Ethics Law Reform agreed that pro bono work or murky cases of deferred or indirect compensation raise the same danger of improper influence as work that is directly compensated.[5]

The federal law does not affect employees in the process of leaving the private sector to enter government service. Therefore, the "golden handshake," a large bonus or severance benefit to the departing employee, is permitted. Melvin Paisley, a key figure in a Defense Department contractors' scandal, received benefits worth $183,000 when he left the Boeing Company in 1981 to joint the Navy as a procurement officer.[6] In a unanimous decision, the Supreme Court held that Boeing's payment to Paisley and four other executives entering government service did not violate the federal law.[7]

Golden handshakes may or may not buy actual influence over the new government employee, but they carry a strong appearance of impropriety. Certain benefits earned during the private employment, such as pension funds, should not be forfeited upon entering government, but it is improper for the prospective public employee to accept any bonus or severance benefit that was not earned during private employment.

Restrictions on federal employees begin by prohibiting their participation in a matter involving a person or organization with whom they are negotiating or have an arrangement about prospective employment. The President's commission recommended extending that prohibition to all members of Congress and employees of the legislative and judicial branches.[8]

After they leave for private jobs, former employees are forbidden to participate in or attempt to influence any matter "in which he participated personally or substantially as an officer or employee through decision, approval, disapproval, recommendation, the rendering of advice, investigation or otherwise" while in government.[9]

Next, former government employees are prohibited for two years after their employment ends from appearing in or attempting to influence (or helping others to do so) matters that were pending under their responsibility within the last year of employment or in which they participated personally and substantially.[10] Finally, former employees are prohibited from appearing before the department or agency in which they served for one year.[11] This one year cooling-off period currently applies only to designated senior employees of the executive branch, although both the Senate and House rules contain that bar. The President's commission recommended extending it to all members of the legislative and judicial branches and their senior staff.[12]

The other loophole addressed by the President's commission was the compartmentalization of the White House that allowed, for example, a former Deputy Chief of Staff to lobby the Director of the Office of Management and Budget before one year elapsed because the President's staff and the OMB were treated as different agencies, even though officials in each worked together closely. (Former Reagan aide Michael Deaver was not prosecuted for violating the revolving door prohibitions, but for lying about his conduct.) The commission recommended treating the Executive Office of the President as one agency, rather than the nine discrete agencies now recognized for purposes of the cooling-off period.[13]

The maximum penalty for violating the Ethics in Government Act is imprisonment for one year, unless the conduct was willful, in which case the maximum is imprisonment for five years.[14] In addition, the violator may be penalized as much as $50,000 for each violation or the amount received for the violation, whichever is greater.[15] The act applies only to the executive branch and independent agencies, not to Congress. Former

representatives and senators are not restrained in a new career as lobbyists. In fact, few legislators become lobbyists and few lobbyists have
served as legislators, fewer than 3 percent in Washington and fewer than
10 percent at the state level.

EXPERIENCE WANTED

Shortly after becoming general counsel to the Federal Deposit Insurance
Corporation, John Douglas began receiving calls from headhunters eager
to grab a high government banking lawyer for their law firm or corporate
clients. While some government lawyers command huge salaries in private
practice, others must be able to show that they can bring in clients: this
is not a skill developed in government service. For technocrats or administrative positions, the government experience alone is the
qualification.

The legislative revolving door primarily involves staffers. Key congressional aides and committee employees have the same inside knowledge
and influence as agency employees. Even though they do not directly
vote on legislation, their role in the drafting of legislation and the oversight
work of congressional committees is equally valuable to industry. Increasingly, staff work is the way to prepare for the much more lucrative
lobbying career.

Shortly before leaving office, President Reagan vetoed a bill that would
have essentially applied the Ethics in Government Act to former lawmakers and top aides and extended the ban on executive branch officials
to prevent them from representing foreign countries or foreign-owned
companies. The House voted 374 to 19 in favor of the bill. The President
termed it "excessive and discriminatory."[16] He also raised the argument
applied to all revolving door legislation that qualified people decline to
enter government because they would be slightly restricted when they
returned to private jobs. An ethical former public official will be even
more cautious than the law would have required. Other ethical restraints,
such as full financial disclosure, will discourage only a few qualified people
from entering public life. Bluntly put, we can get along without those who
are unwilling to avoid conflicts of interest and the appearance of
impropriety.

One revolving door abuse not addressed by the present law is the use
of nonclassified, but nonpublic information by former employees. Even
though the former employee does not engage in any representation prohibited by the law, there is no restriction on the use of information acquired while in government service in behind-the-scenes work other than
restrictions concerning classified information. There is a great deal of
valuable but confidential information that is not classified. In the field of
government procurement or international trade and finance, the kind of

information that would be considered proprietary in the private sector has tremendous value. The President's Commission on Federal Ethics Law Reform recommended former employees be forbidden to disclose such information for a period of two years.[17] After two years, most confidential information would be stale.

The commission recognized the problem of adequately defining *nonpublic information* if criminal penalties were to be assessed. In formulating an ethical rule, the standard need not be quite so exacting: It is unethical for former public employees to gain an advantage from the use of information obtained in government service that was not available to the public at the time. Ethical concerns do not disappear at the end of any arbitrary time period, and mere compliance with the law recommended by the President's commission would not be the same as acting ethically under the circumstances.

With few exceptions, state and local governments do not restrict former employees from representing business interests before their former employer, government agencies. There are obviously more former employees and more opportunities for undue influence at those levels of government: there is also less scrutiny of the decisions made there. The need for ethical self-restraint is even greater in that environment.

ETHICAL GUIDELINES

1. Public officials should only seek or retain their positions based on a proper motive to serve the legitimate ends of government, rather than to accumulate excessive personal wealth or influence.

2. Persons may enter government service intending to stay for only a limited period of time in order to gain a greater knowledge of government generally or of a particular agency *or* to lend their expertise at higher levels within government. In any case, they should commit themselves to a reasonable period of time in that position, so that wasteful turnover is minimized and they can make a meaningful contribution to government service.

3. Employees leaving private industry for government service should refuse any severance benefits or "golden handshakes" that were not earned during the private employment.

4. Public officials who leave government service should not seek employment or clients with any promise, express or implied, that they have informal access or influence because of their prior experience. They should not take advantage of the access or influence that they do have to obtain information or action for themselves, private employers, or clients to which others are not equally entitled.

5. Former public officials should not use information obtained in government service that was not available to the public at the time.

6. Public officials should treat former colleagues who are now in the private sector on the same terms as any other person with whom the official deals. Officials should be aware that there is an appearance of impropriety from any informality or cooperation accorded to former colleagues, even if others would have been treated equally.

NOTES

1. Archibald Cox, Chairman of Common Cause, Testimony Before Subcomm. on Oversight of Gov't. Management of the Senate Governmental Affairs Committee, Apr. 12, 1988 [quoted in McBride, *Ethics in Congress: Agenda and Action*, 58 GEO. WASH. L. REV. 451 (1990)].

2. Machan, *Costly but Priceless*, Forbes, Nov. 28, 1988, at 266, 267.

3. Forbes, *Facts and Comment*, Forbes, Apr. 3, 1989, at 19.

4. 18 U.S.C. 207 (1988).

5. Recommendation 15, TO SERVE WITH HONOR: REPORT OF THE PRESIDENT'S COMMISSION ON FEDERAL ETHICS LAW REFORM, Mar. 1989, at 77–78.

6. Herbers, *Demand for Ethics in Government Has Outstripped Supply*, N.Y. Times, June 6, 1988, at 4, col. 1.

7. *Boeing v. United States*, 494 U.S. 152, 110 S.Ct. 997, 108 L.Ed. 2d 132 (1990).

8. Recommendation 9, *supra* note 5.

9. 18 U.S.C. 207(a)(3) (1988).

10. 18 U.S.C. 207(b) (1988).

11. 18 U.S.C. 207(c) (1988).

12. Recommendation 10, *supra* note 5.

13. Recommendation 14, *supra* note 5.

14. 18 U.S.C. 216(a) (1990).

15. 18 U.S.C. 216(b) (1990).

16. Yang, *Reagan Will Veto Ethics Measure: President Calls Bill Discriminatory*, Wall St. J., Oct. 24, 1988, at 8, col. 6.

17. Recommendation 11, *supra* note 5.

Lawyers in Public Life

When people gather to swap lawyer stories, they pick on a group in American life that, according to polls, is not widely admired. (However, most of them would be quite pleased if one of their children entered the legal profession.) They may tell about the sharks who not only passed up the chance to eat a lawyer but even gave him a ride to shore—all in the name of professional courtesy. Shakespeare wrote, "The first thing we do, let's kill all the lawyers."[1] People forget the context of that remark, an effort to overthrow the government. Because lawyers in government protected the status quo, the revolutionaries needed them out of the way.

In this country, lawyers led the revolutionaries. Many colonial leaders and signers of the Declaration of Independence were lawyers. Except for Washington, most prominent early Presidents and national legislators were lawyers. The dominance of American government by lawyers has continued. The lawyerly personality is suited to political combat. Knowledge of the law is invaluable in proposing and passing legislation.

Lawyers are also well suited to be lobbyists. Because many legislators are lawyers, the lawyer-lobbyist knows how to communicate with them and can speak with more credibility about legal issues in proposed legislation. Lobbying is a major function of many Washington D.C., law firms, some of which do nothing else. One phone call from Lloyd Cutler or Clark Clifford, who have the added benefit of lengthy political and governmental experience, may be better than an army of lobbyists. In the first quarter of 1991, California lawyer-lobbyists earned $3.8 million in lobbying fees.

TWO SETS OF ETHICS

Lawyers in government are bound by two sets of ethics: those ethical principles which should be followed by all public officials and codes of legal ethics, which have provisions specific to governmental service. The Code of Professional Responsibility organizes the ethics of current and former government lawyers in three ways. First, the general statement in Canon 8, "A lawyer should assist in improving the legal system." Second, there are several ethical considerations (ECs), which are aspirational statements. For example,

EC 8–1: . . . By reason of education and experience, lawyers are especially qualified to recognize deficiencies in the legal system and to initiate corrective measures therein. Thus they should participate in proposing and supporting legislation and programs to improve the system, without regard to the general interests or desires of clients or former clients.

EC 8–4: Whenever a lawyer seeks legislative or administrative changes, he should identify the capacity in which he appears, whether on behalf of himself, a client, or the public. A lawyer may advocate such changes on behalf of a client even though he does not agree with them. But when a lawyer purports to act on behalf of the public, he should espouse only those changes which he conscientiously believes to be in the public interest.

EC 8–5: Fraudulent, deceptive, or otherwise illegal conduct by a participant in a proceeding before a tribunal or legislative body is inconsistent with fair administration of justice, and it should never be participated in or condoned by lawyers. Unless constrained by his obligations to preserve the confidences and secrets of his client, a lawyer should reveal to appropriate authorities any knowledge he may have of such improper conduct.

EC 8–8: Lawyers often serve as legislators or as holders of other public offices. This is highly desirable, as lawyers are uniquely qualified to make significant contributions to the improvement of the legal system. A lawyer who is a public officer, whether full or part-time, should not engage in activities in which his personal or professional interests are or forseeably may be in conflict with his official duties.

Finally, the Code of Professional Responsibility contains disciplinary rules (DRs), violations of which are punishable by the state's lawyer disciplinary system. DR 8–101, *Action as a Public Official*, provides that a lawyer who holds public office shall not:

(1) Use his public position to obtain, or attempt to obtain, a special advantage in legislative matters for himself or for a client under circumstances where he knows or it is obvious that such action is not in the public interest.

(2) Use his public position to influence, or attempt to influence, a tribunal to act in favor of himself or of a client.

(3) Accept any thing of value from any person when the lawyer knows or it is obvious that the offer is for the purpose of influencing his actions as a public official.

Lawyer-lobbyists face ethical dilemmas when one client hires them to support or oppose a bill that conflicts with the interests of another client. If both clients hire the lawyer to lobby, the conflict is obvious. If the conflict is between the lobbying client and a client whom they represent in litigation or business planning, the conflict may not be so obvious. California lawyer-lobbyist Thomas E. Bone said, ''We are very cautious about [conflicts] when we are approached by a client. We run them through in-house mechanics, pen memos to other members, and run computer checks of all clients and issues. When you do that thorough a job, frequently you'll find a conflict. So you'll have to deal with it somehow, or refuse to take the client.''[2] One way to deal with it is to seek a waiver, after receiving full advice, by both clients giving the lawyer permission to continue representing them both.

Lawyers who are also public officials have greater ethical restrictions. For example, other legislators may be free under state law to accept gifts under circumstances where the lawyer-legislator must refuse them. In general, lawyers involved in public life or who deal with government should be more concerned with the public good and full disclosure.

THE FIRST TEMPTATION OF LAWYERS

Most lawyers establish a practice by becoming well known in the community. Traditionally, the best way to gain clients has been the visibility of politics. Far more people see political candidates and officeholders perform than will watch a lawyer in the courtroom or advising clients in the law office. The benefits from general publicity and from doing a good job in public life are well deserved.

The danger is that clients will hire a lawyer who is also a public official or a law firm that has connections with a public official in an effort to gain influence over the official's decision making. Lawyers who are also public officials should not solicit business from companies or individuals who have obvious legislative or administrative needs. Nor should they accept fees from any client who is directly affected by pending legislation or executive decision in which the lawyer-official may be involved.

Clients who seek out the lawyer-legislator or her law firm for an improper reason rarely advertise the fact. Their approach may be subtle or directed to legal work that presents no conceiveable conflict. But by building loyalty and a certain dependence or gratitude for his business, the client collects IOUs, which may be called in the future. When new companies come to town, they seem to pick the law firm with the best political connections. Clients should be told at the outset that no influence on the public official will result from the representation and that if a specific conflict arises between the client's interest and the need for the attorney to be an ethical public official, the client will have to find a new lawyer.

One profile in courage is North Carolina State Senator and majority leader Tony Rand, whose law firm had been retained to represent the railroad company CSX Transportation. The company fired the law firm because Senator Rand had taken "positions antagonistic to the railroad." One editorial said, "Apparently CSX thought it had bought something that Senator Rand wasn't selling: His vote in the General Assembly." The company's action would have also violated a state law against threatening a legislator with economic reprisal, except that it acted after the vote rather than before.

A final overlap between law, politics, and ethics is the rise in lawyer PACs. During 1989–90, the Association of Trial Lawyers of America PAC raised almost $4 million. The largest law firm PAC was the Cleveland-based, national firm Jones, Day, Reavis & Pogue, which raised almost $600,000.[3] The use of lawyer PAC money to back up lobbying on issues affecting the legal profession leads to the same problems of real and apparent conflicts of interest as any other PAC. When a bill is introduced in Congress, either narrowing or expanding a legal field like products liability, it is called a "cash cow." Business PACs line up on one side, while lawyer PACs line up on the other.

PROSECUTORS

A prosecutor is both a public official and a lawyer. Elected prosecutors are also politicians. Beginning as a prosecutor and succeeding with a high-profile case has been a starting point for many political careers. The pressures are enormous to play to the public and conduct the office with a view to the political future. However, an ethical prosecutor does not allow political considerations to influence prosecutorial decisions. Prosecutors have great discretion in what charges to bring against a defendant, which investigations to push, and whether to pursue cases of political corruption. That discretion must be exercised with a sense of both justice and mercy, but without regard to how the prosecutor's political fortunes are affected.

A prosecutor's duty is not to seek convictions but to seek justice. Under the pressures of their office, particularly if it is an elected one, the zeal to convict and make headlines overpowers the ethical duty. Harvard law professor Alan Dershowitz said,

Selective leaks to the media have become a conventional weapon in the prosecutorial arsenal. My friends in the press confirm what every defense attorney already knows: that some prosecutors and journalists have developed a symbiotic relationship built on the mutual benefit each derives when the press publishes a scoop based on grand jury proceedings or other supposedly secret investigations.

The level above local prosecutors is the state attorney general. The Josephson Institute's Government Ethics Center summarized three ethical obligations of those statewide prosecutors:

I.   The attorney general must assure that lawyers in the attorney general's office render competent professional service.

II. The attorney general must assure that the office zealously advocates the interests of the people of the state within the bounds of law and propriety.

III. The attorney general must assure that lawyers in the office do not engage in professional or private conduct that will undermine public respect for lawyers or confidence in the commitment of the government to assure all citizens equal justice under the law.[4]

Because state attorneys general handle a broader range of cases than local district attorneys, they are subject to different political pressure. They represent the Governor and state agencies in disputes with private persons or groups and other levels of government. Yet the Governor or the agency head is not their client. The people of the state are all clients. When a state official's conduct or legal claims conflict with the best interests of the people, the attorney general should resolve the conflict of interest in favor of the higher duty to the people.

Federal prosecutors, headed by the Attorney General of the United States, have even greater power than local district attorneys. Furthermore, the Attorney General and the Department of Justice are symbols for the ordered rule of law. Former Attorney General Griffin Bell, also the Vice Chairman of the President's Commission on Federal Ethics Law Reform, wrote about his goal on becoming Attorney General:

My desire to bolster the public's confidence in federal prosecutors was part of a larger concern about the way in which the Justice Department had been used—and abused—in the recent past. That the attorney general be free from political influence is essential to public confidence in his office. The Watergate scandal and the corrosive effect it had on the public's faith in the honesty of government resulted partly from the fact that two consecutive attorneys general [John Mitchell and Richard Kleindienst] failed to exercise independent judgment and engaged in questionable practices.[5]

JUDGES ARE LAWYERS, TOO

Judges have greater power over people than prosecutors and greater power than legislators, who cannot act without the votes of others. Judges are governed by a Code of Judicial Conduct that regulates ethical use of their power. A subcommittee of the America Bar Association is currently revising that code. The revolving door phenomenon discussed in Chapter 9 is seen less frequently in the judicial branch. Perhaps with the threatened resignations of underpaid judges, it will become more common. The President's Commission on Federal Ethics Law Reform recommended that judges be prohibited from appearing before the court over which they presided for a cooling-off period for one year.

The Ethics Reform Act of 1989 applied some restrictions that make more sense in the legislative and executive branches to judges. For example, the ban on honoraria for all but the Senate means that a federal judge cannot teach without approval of the Judicial Conference and that the cap on teaching pay is well below what a law school would normally pay an adjunct professor.[6] Also, a judge cannot be compensated for writing or speaking, even when the work would benefit the legal profession or the court system.

The rules of judicial ethics assume that the popular election of judges will continue. The wisdom of that procedure is challenged by the Texas state Supreme Court's refusal to hear an appeal of Pennzoil's $10.3 billion judgment against Texaco. Pennzoil's lawyers had contributed more than $355,000 to the election campaigns of the Texas Supreme Court justices.[7] In fact, one of the issues on appeal was the trial judge's acceptance of a $10,000 campaign contribution from Pennzoil's lead trial lawyer.[8]

The former Texas Chief Justice, John Hill, resigned to lead the fight to abolish the election of judges. He had spent more than $1 million to be elected in 1984, and two candidates to succeed him planned to spend $1.5 million each for election efforts. Texas is not unique. In Ohio, the 1986 race for its Supreme Court Chief Justice cost $2.7 million, up from less than $100,000 in 1980.

Only eight states continue to elect all judges. But about one-half of all state judges run for election initially or must campaign to retain their seats. The main source of campaign funds are the lawyers and law firms who appear before the judges. Also, special interest groups have discovered the state supreme courts make many public policy decisions. It is cheaper to influence those elections than legislative or gubernatorial races. Ethical considerations about campaign financing apply to judges, with the additional rule that contributions from persons or lawyers with cases pending before the judge should be refused.

The rules of judicial ethics prohibit a judge running for election from making any comments on legal or political issues. It has been suggested that a judge's campaign slogan must be "I'll be fair. (That's all I can say.)" Aside from First Amendment concerns about limiting any person's right to speak about matters of legitimate public concern, it is especially important to know the judge's general legal and political philosophy, even though the judge should not be asked about specific cases. The confirmation process for Supreme Court Justices is a better approach. Most nominees are willing to make broad statements about their views but avoid applying them to hypothetical or real cases. If a nominee (or judicial candidate) refuses to state general beliefs about the law, that is a reason to vote against that prospective jurist.

Judicial elections rarely provide real choices. Typically the vote is strictly based on incumbency or party membership. Rarely do the voters recognize any judge's name. A study in Texas showed that only 14.5 percent of those leaving a polling place could remember the name of one state supreme court or appeals court candidate, compared to 43.7 percent who could remember a senate candidate and 50.7 who could remember the name of a candidate for the House of Representatives. Only 2.5 percent could recall the name of a county court candidate, and only 4.9 percent could recall the name of district court candidates.[9]

The trend is toward less partisan methods of selecting and retaining judges in office. Merit selection by public panels is more likely to result in qualified, impartial judges. Another difference is that minority judges are more likely to come from merit selection than by elections. The screening process typically selects a small group of qualified applicants from which the governor or senator can choose. That protects the official from offending anyone deemed unqualified, although he or she must still make a political choice among the qualified candidates. The current ethical ban on announcing his or her views on legal and political issues also applies to the merit selection process.

After a judge is appointed following merit selection, elections should affect only the retention of judges. If a judge loses the public's confidence, he or she can be voted out. The replacement is not an election opponent but another person approved by the selection panel.

ETHICAL GUIDELINES

1. Lawyers who are also public officials should comply with standards of public service ethics, as well as codes of legal ethics. They must be especially sensitive to avoid the appearance of impropriety.

2. While it is permissible to represent clients attracted to a lawyer-official because of the official's public service, clients must be told that no influence on public business will be permitted and that if a specific conflict of interest develops, the client must seek new representation.

3. Prosecutors are bound by standards of public service ethics, as well as codes of legal ethics, and should exercise their discretion and power over people objectively, without regard to political considerations.

4. Judges should strictly comply with the Code of Judicial Conduct and absolutely avoid the appearance of impropriety. If their office is elective,

they should refuse all campaign contributions from parties or lawyers in pending cases, as well as any contribution intended to buy influence over future cases.

NOTES

1. W. Shakespeare, HENRY VI, PART II, IV.ii.86.

2. Hallye Jordan, *Split Loyalties Mean a Thin Ethics Line*, L.A. Daily J., Apr. 18, 1991, at 11.

3. MacLachlan, *Lawyer PACs Pack Wallop*, NAT'L L.J., Apr. 22, 1991, at 3.

4. ETHICAL OBLIGATIONS AND OPPORTUNITIES FOR ATTORNEYS GENERAL, Josephon Inst. Gov't. Ethics Center, Dec. 1988, at 29.

5. G. Bell, TAKING CARE OF THE LAW 182 (1989).

6. *Interview: Judge Frank Coffin: Working to Improve the Status of Federal Judges*, The Third Branch 11 (1989).

7. *Campaign Practices in Judges' Elections Spark Drive for Merit Appointments in Pennsylvania*, Wall St. J., Dec. 9, 1988, at A16, col. 1.

8. *Texaco, Inc. v. Pennzoil Co.*, 784 F.2d 1133 (1986).

9. Campagne & Thielmann, *Awareness of Trial Court Judges*, 74 JUDICATURE 271 (Feb.–Mar. 1991).

11

The Private Lives of
Public Officials

When this chapter was first drafted, the media was reporting the marital infidelity of San Antonio Mayor Henry Cisneros and Nancy Reagan's permanent "borrowing" of expensive designer gowns. Shortly before, we learned about Gary Hart's private morality, the complicated personal financial dealings of U.S. Attorney General Edwin Meese, and the gambling habits of Louisiana Governor Edwin Edwards, who said he could only lose an election if he were caught in bed with a dead woman or a live man. In early 1989, rumors about Senator John Tower's personal life scuttled his nomination as Secretary of Defense, despite his extraordinary pledge to abstain from alcohol if confirmed.[1]

When you read this book, there will be a new list of names and transgressions. While there is no evidence that Americans have suddenly become puritanical, the standards for the private conduct of government officials have risen just as surely as ethics in public life. In addition, people such as New Right activist Paul Weyrich argue that certain positions are so sensitive and important (President, Secretary of State, Secretary of Defense, CIA Director) that standards even higher than for other public officials are justified.[2]

Modern politicians do not react like Alabama's Big Jim Folsom, who admitted to all accusations and tried to exaggerate them. He said, "Ain't no use denying it if they're accusing you of something. Always enlarge on it, especially if it ain't so. You go to denying somethin', they'll say, hell, he's guilty."

Are public officials entitled to have private lives? Do their human fail-
ings in private life affect their ability to serve responsibly and ethically
in office? A *Wall Street Journal*/NBC News poll in mid–1991 showed that
the public believed that the press legitimately reported on John Sununu's
government airplane rides and ethics allegations regarding New York
Senator D'Amato. However, a clear majority believed that the press had
gone too far in publicizing allegations about Virginia Senator Charles
Robb's private life and various Kennedy family members accused of personal misconduct in Florida.[3]

Muckraking is a long-standing practice in journalism. George Washington said, "The eyes of Argus are upon me; no slip will pass unnoticed."
Even if you wanted to believe the worst about Nancy Reagan, it is hard
to do so based on the anonymous journalism that sells well on supermarket
racks. Norman J. Orenstein, a resident scholar at the American Enterprise
Institute, says that journalists are now willing to print any salacious report
about a public figure. The new standard he sees is: "We just heard a hint
about an innuendo about a rumor—go with it above the fold, and forget
the caveats."

Reacting to nude photos of Prince Andrew, the chief of the British Press
Complaints Commission said, "The public interest is not defined as what
is interesting to the public." Because we lack a royal family in this country, only entertainment stars receive more scrutiny of their off-duty conduct than do political figures. A few politicians act like the man who said,
"I spent most of my money on booze and women, and the rest of it I just
wasted." It is hard to sympathize with the public official who seeks publicity but cannot avoid the private misconduct that may be uncovered as
a result. (Gary Hart's invitation to the press to follow him and see that
he was doing nothing wrong will be added to those lists of the world's
worst decisions.) And the stern, self-righteous official caught in an em-
barrassing but private mistake may deserve ridicule.

This chapter is about mundane examples at all levels of government:
the sheriff whose son has a drug problem, the senator who was treated
for mental illness, a homosexual public official, the mayor whose husband
participates in financial scams and hovers near bankruptcy. Because none
of us live perfect lives or belong to perfect families, certain private matters
should remain private, or we will lose the services of an unacceptable
number of good public servants. Does it matter that a presidential candidate's wife was pregnant before their marriage or that a senator exper-
imented with marijuana while in college?

However, the distinction between private and public life for elected
officials or appointees to high posts is different than for the rest of us.
The public is entitled to know if the official is distracted to the extent that
his or her work suffers or if a family member or business associate creates
a conflict of interest. The duty is first on the official to disclose to the

public when a private matter affects his public responsibilities. If she chooses not to do so or if he cannot recognize the problem, responsible media or other citizens should publicize it.

Only those private indiscretions or family problems which may affect performance of the public job need to be publicly known. Otherwise private problems can affect job performance if, for example, the official must devote extraordinary time to it. An illness in the family is purely personal, unless the official is so consumed with helping or being with the family member that the public's work is neglected. The fact that Kitty Dukakis is an alcoholic and that an illness involved her drinking rubbing alcohol was important to the people of Massachusetts when Michael Dukakis was Governor, even though her husband lost the presidential race.

The difficult question remains: Is it fair to ask more of our leaders than we live up to ourselves? Walter Lippmann wrote,

Those in high places are more than the administrators of government bureaus. They are more than the writers of laws They are the custodians of a nation's ideals, of the beliefs it cherishes, of its permanent hopes, of the faith which makes a nation out of a mere aggregation of individuals.[4]

HEALTH

An official's illness or disease is a purely private concern, unless it impairs performance or is potentially incapacitating. The public's legitimate interest in the health of local or elected officials is usually slight. We pay much more attention to the President's health. The deception of the public about the health of Woodrow Wilson and Franklin Roosevelt is astonishing by modern standards. The public was entitled to know more about President Dwight Eisenhower's medical condition. After the attempted assassination of President Reagan, his courage and good humor masked the seriousness of his injury, which may have justified invoking the Twenty-fifth Amendment's temporary transfer of power.

The ethical duty to release all relevant medical details means that the public has a right to know more than it may actually want to know. After the extensive medical reporting of President Reagan's various surgeries, drive-in theater critic Joe Bob Briggs spoke for many people when he said, "I don't want to hear anymore about Ronald Reagan's gizzards. That's disgusting."

FINANCES

Not a few statesmen have been prevented from boldly and honestly taking that course which their genius or inmost and genuine bias of soul and sympathy pointed out to them, solely because they were

indebted, first in a pecuniary way, and consequently by way of gratitude or decency, to those who assisted them. It is not necessary that
they actually sell their better judgment; the worst effect of continued
straitened circumstances is that they affect unconsciously even the
nobler minds.

—Francis Lieber, *Manual of Political Ethics* (1838)

Personal financial failures by public officials are not new. Lincoln was
abysmal in business dealings. It took Harry Truman more than twenty
years to pay off creditors of his failed haberdashery shop. Although some
of the best public servants were business successes, others sought public
office after it was clear they had no future in the private sector. Private
financial troubles have public implications in two ways. First, if the official
has budgetary responsibility or public financial control, the inability to
master personal finances is a reliable, if not perfect, indication that the
public finances may be mismanaged. Second, a person with severe money
troubles may be more tempted by improper influences or an opportunity
to embezzle.

Public officials who cannot manage personal finances may do a fine job
with the public's money and never steal or take bribes. However, because
the concern is legitimate, the public has a right to know. New York Mayor
David Dinkins was elected despite his failure to pay income tax for four
years and his $58,000 sale to his son of stock that he valued two years
earlier at $1 million.

As discussed in Chapter 4, full financial disclosure, including the release
of tax returns, is ethically necessary, even though the law may require
less. A candidate's willingness to disclose financial data ought to be an
important voting point with the public. Although legislators do not have
budgetary responsibilities, a troubled financial past suggests a greater
temptation to act unethically with special interests or lobbyists.

Complete financial disclosure may discourage successful people from
seeking public office, not because of financial difficulties, but because of
business relationships with others who do not want their affairs disclosed.
Today, a candidate's finances may be honestly and competently handled
but complicated. That is unfortunate, but it is an acceptable disadvantage.
Furthermore, those situations can be minimized. The desire to seek public
office rarely hits a person like a thunderbolt. Rather, men and women
with a desire to enter public life can begin disentangling themselves over
a period of time from business relationships they would be reluctant to
publicize, instead of losing money by a last-minute liquidation. In many
cases, they can arrange their finances in advance. To the extent that they
thereby lose business opportunities, they must decide whether the satisfactions of public service outweigh the possible monetary loss.

Public officials can minimize financial conflicts of interest and the appearance of impropriety by putting substantial assets in a blind trust. As discussed in Chapter 8, a truly blind trust gives the trustee complete power over the assets, and the public official is only given information about the performance of the trust, not its holdings. There are circumstances where the asset is, for example, a family business that the official would not want sold. Any restrictions on the trustee's powers should be publicly disclosed so that the public can evaluate whether a conflict of interest continues to exist.

SEXUAL MISCONDUCT

The most titillating, but least relevant, issues in the private lives of prominent public officials involve sex. Frequently, sexual misconduct is merely the symptom of another problem that may directly affect job performance. When the powerful Arkansas Representative Wilbur Mills was caught dancing in a fountain with a stripper or when Gary Hart sailed on *Monkey Business*, we wanted to know all the juicy details. The underlying alcoholism of Wilbur Mills may have had much more to do with his performance as Chairman of the Ways and Means Committee than whatever happened in the fountain. If so, that was the real story. Gary Hart's invitation to the press to catch him in an impropriety may have demonstrated a danger-seeking or self-destructive trait more significant than the impropriety that was disclosed.

In 1989, the House Ethics Committee was investigating the sexual behavior of four sitting members. While Massachusetts Representative Gerry Studds was easily reelected after revelations that he had sex with a male congressional page, another Massachusetts Representative, Barney Frank, was devastated by continual publicity of new sexual misconduct charges. Perhaps the dirtiest recent smear was committed by the Republican National Committee staffer who wrote a memo titled "Tom Foley: Out of the Liberal Closet." It compared Foley's voting record with Frank's but implied that they shared the same sexual preference. The staffer was fired. As Senator Bob Dole said about the memo, "This is not politics, this is garbage."

Just a few years ago, divorce would have ended a political career. President Kennedy's reportedly numerous sexual adventures may have been well known to insiders but might have led to his impeachment at the time if publicly known. When private sexual conduct does not bear on the official's honesty or competence, it should remain private. The pain caused to the family is great enough without the added pain of publicity. Some will argue that any sexual misconduct is relevant to the official's honesty or competence. The line is hard to draw. Any display of poor judgment in private life may indicate a potential for poor judgment in office. However, John Kennedy's private lapses do not seem to have detracted from his conduct of his public duties. With most public officials, exposure of isolated, atypical moral failures that do not affect their job performance is an unjustified invasion of the privacy to which even public officials are entitled.

THE APPEARANCE OF IMPROPRIETY

Even where public officials have a zone of privacy, they must be sensitive about the need to avoid the appearance of impropriety. After the accusations of misconduct fill the front pages, rebuttals and retractions will be buried in the back by the furniture ads. The public official whose private life is unfairly disclosed is in a poor position to complain. Any objection sounds like whining. Only a political friend will come to his defense, but that is so expected as to be ineffective. Like the risk of financial loss, public service will cause a loss of privacy in any event and, perhaps an unfair loss. Harry Truman's advice assumes that the world is unfair: "If you can't stand the heat, stay out of the kitchen."

During the attention focused on former Speaker Wright's mistakes, it became known that his chief aide, John P. Mack, had been convicted for a savage knife attack on a woman sixteen years before. There was no question that he had been an honest and competent staffer whose crime was related in no way to his government service. Although there were other, conflicting allegations, Mack resigned.[5] He was either a victim of pressures to get rid of his boss or another example of Harry Truman's rule.

ETHICAL GUIDELINES

1. Only those private indiscretions or family problems which might reasonably affect the public official's job performance should be publicly disclosed. If the official does not voluntarily disclose those relevant public matters, the media or other citizens have a duty to investigate and report them.

2. The public has a right to know about a public official's serious illness or injury. Candidates for major full-time public offices should disclose serious health problems before seeking election or appointment.

3. Public officials should arrange personal financial affairs so that job performance is not impaired and possible conflicts of interest are minimized. Wealthy full-time officials should create blind trusts that free them from all concern for preserving their wealth.

4. Public officials should lead exemplary personal lives in order to avoid the appearance of impropriety. The public has a right to know about private moral failures that suggest character defects or conflicts of interest that may affect the official's judgment or job performance.

NOTES

1. *The Nunn Standard*, Wall St. J., Feb. 28, 1989, at A20, col. 1.

2. Weyrich, *Private Affairs and Public Interests*, Wall St. J., Feb. 27, 1989, at A10, col. 4.

3. Shribman, *Public Backs Inquiries of Official Acts by Politicians, Not Their Private Lives*, Wall. St. J., May 17, 1991, at A16, col. 1.

4. Lippmann quoted in Reston, *Private Behavior, Public Responsibility*, N.Y. Times, Dec. 25, 1987, at 27, col. 2.

5. Karnish, *Wright Aide Quits amid Questions of Crime*, Boston Globe May 12, 1989, at 3 (nat'l./foreign ed.)

12

Enforcing Ethics

In the Teapot Dome scandal of the 1920s, Interior Secretary Albert Fall secretly leased navy oil reserves to companies from which he received "loans." Eventually, he was convicted for taking bribes. Almost seventy years later, former HUD Secretary Samuel Pierce became the first cabinet officer since Albert Fall to take the Fifth Amendment before a congressional investigating committee. Pierce was certainly entitled to exercise his constitutional right to silence, and his culpability, if any, may not match Fall's. However, both cases exemplify ineffective, inefficient efforts to enforce public ethics.

Codes of public service ethics that are only aspirational are, of course, better than nothing. Ideally, a code of ethics will have teeth in it. If part of a legal code, it will provide an enforcement mechanism. Every level and branch of government should adopt tough ethical standards with the force of law.

The enforcement of public service ethics should occur along two separate tracks. For elected and appointed state officials, there should be an independent, statewide ethics commission with broad enforcement powers that conducts its activities publicly. New York Attorney General Robert Abrams proposed that New York enforce public service ethics

by creating a single, highly visible body to which the public can turn with suspicions of wrongdoing within government. . . . The very existence of a New York

State Ethics Commission, armed with the power to subpoena witnesses and compel testimony and equipped with adequate staff and budget resources, would send a clear message to the public that corruption of any kind and at any level of government *will not be tolerated.*

Ethical guidelines, such as those in this book, can be enforced by such a commission. However, the primary duties of such commissions will be the enforcement of much more specific campaign financing, reporting, and disclosure laws, as well as continuing conflict of interest regulations and lobbyist disclosure. We have tried to avoid the level of detail that should be considered for such a public, statewide enforcement apparatus.

A similar federal ethics commission should enforce the ethics laws of elected and appointed federal officials. The President's Commission on Federal Ethics Law Reform recommended that the existing Office of Government Ethics consolidate all executive branch ethics standards into a comprehensive manual.[1] It also recommended that Congress appoint an independent ethics official, confirmed by both houses, to head a permanent ethics office to investigate alleged misconduct, publicly report its findings, and recommend appropriate sanctions.[2] Whether the executive and legislative ethics enforcement proceeds separately or together, the ethics agencies need real power.

When they have power, we should expect them to use it when justified, rather than merely slapping wrists. The California Fair Political Practices Commission recently fined the state's Transportation Commissioner $165,000 for voting on San Diego County freeway projects when it was likely that the winning contractors would rent or buy heavy equipment from the Commissioner's Caterpillar dealership.[3]

After the Senate Ethics Committee tapped the wrists of four of the Keating Five, a good news/bad news joke circulated in Washington. The good news was that Saddam Hussein would be tried for war crimes. The bad news was that the Senate Ethics Committee would be the judges.

The basic problem with the perception that justified discipline was not meted out is the conflict of interest that exists when sitting legislators are asked to punish their colleagues. Nor do they enjoy it. In a recent one-year period there was complete turnover on the House Ethics Committee and nearly complete turnover on the Senate Ethics Committee. Norman Ornstein suggests using congressmen emeriti on the ethics panel.[4] Former members of either chamber would know the practical problems facing those accused of ethics violations but would not be troubled by the prospect of imposing sanctions. Doing so would not hamper the retired members' political career or legislative goals.

Violations of the laws that state or federal ethics commissions monitor would be referred for prosecution, in addition to the sanctions, such as fines or suspensions, that the commission would be empowered to impose.

Part of the enforcement process at the federal level involves the use of special prosecutors, also known as independent counsel, to investigate criminal misconduct by executive branch officials. Those officials include the President, the Vice President, Cabinet-level officials, senior White House aides, top Justice Department officials, the CIA Director or Deputy Director, the IRS Commissioner, and managers of national campaigns or national campaign committees. The law includes a cumbersome procedure to initiate the special prosecution effort, but the law itself has withstood legal challenges. In *Morrison v. Olson*, the Supreme Court upheld the constitutionality of court-appointed special prosecutors.[5]

The President's commission recommended that the independent counsel function be expanded to cover members of Congress.[6] The original reason for that law was a lack of credibility when the executive branch investigates itself. On the other hand, there have been numerous successful prosecutions of congressmen by the executive. The commission felt that public confidence in the integrity of justice would be higher if Congress were subject to scrutiny by the independent counsel function.

THE SECOND TRACK

The second, less formal track would enforce ethics throughout government. The enforcement model proposed later in this chapter would work within government agencies and legislative staffs. If not adopted by an entire level of government, it could be self-imposed on branches of government or departments that sought a higher ethical tone. Because most ethics violations reported to an enforcement panel will fall short of criminal conduct, there should be a degree of informality and positive reinforcement to those accused of misconduct.

An informal panel can hear and punish more improper conduct than a court enforcing laws. There is no presumption of innocence before an ethics panel. The standard of proof is not the proof of guilt beyond a reasonable doubt required in criminal cases. Rather, it is the preponderance of the evidence, the standard used in civil lawsuits. In addition, breach of the ethics code by civil servants would be a basis for discipline within the civil service system, as well as discipline or termination for appointees or employees not covered by the civil system.

If an ethics code is adopted, it should designate a government office as the repository for disclosure statements about campaign finances, conflicts of interest, and public officials' financial disclosure forms. Failure to file timely and accurate disclosures would be a breach of the ethics code. Even if the enforcement process is decentralized among different parts of government, accountability is greater if there is a central place for such filings.

The expense of the ethics enforcement process is a legitimate concern when all levels of government face revenue shortfalls. Opponents of an ethics commission in Tennessee raised the issue of the expense of necessary facilities and staff. In fact, its estimated annual cost was 0.004 percent of the state budget. No reasonable ethics enforcement process will present a major budgetary drain. The minimal expense is worth the protection of the public interest.

A code of public service ethics will be more likely to be respected if it is adopted by the consensus of the officials whom it covers than if it is not. If such consensus is not possible, the code should be carefully explained to public employees before it is enforced. Although the President's Commission on Federal Ethics Law Reform was primarily concerned with suggesting new or amended laws, it also recommended that agencies be responsible for the ethics training of employees under the supervision of the Office of Government Ethics.[7] The commission found that

training and education concerning ethical requirements is important to achieve maximum compliance and to minimize the need for sanctions. Leaving responsibility for ethics awareness with the individual agencies will serve to fix accountability on the head of each agency to see that the proper programs are in place and working. . . . Just as important, the Commission believes that the head of each agency should demonstrate his or her commitment to maintaining high ethical standards by personally participating in the agency training program. . . . The example set by the agency head and his senior staff is crucial in setting the tone for ethical behavior by all agency employees.[8]

The California Legislature recently adopted a requirement that legislators, staff members, and lobbyists attend an ethics course each session. Representatives of the Fair Political Practices Commission, the Joint Ethics Committee, and the attorney general's office explained campaign finance, conflict of interest and disclosure laws, and bribery laws. Early reports were that the sessions resembled traffic school, but that they were a worthwhile effort to set a new tone. California Assembly members went through two sessions, conducted by in-house staff, while the state senators participated in a seminar conducted by the Josephson Institute, an ethics center in Los Angeles.

This chapter's enforcement model is a statement of basic principles for either simple or complex efforts at enforcing public service ethics. The Los Angeles City Code of Ethics is the most thorough local government attempt to enforce ethics, but it will draw questions of interpretation for years to come. No code can be drafted to cover all exigencies and answer all questions. But any ethical code, whether formal or informal, should address three enforcement features: reporting, evaluation, and enforcement.

REPORTING

Professional golf is unique among sports because of the self-reporting of infractions of the rules of golf and the self-imposition of penalties, frequently for incidents that no one else noticed. Unfortunately, it is not a realistic approach for public service ethics. Other than unintentional mistakes or harmless errors of judgment, there is little chance that ethical misconduct will be self-reported. However, it is fair to reduce the penalties for violations that are self-reported.

The reporting procedure should be strictly confidential, so that false or malicious reports do not become publicly known and somehow more credible because they are investigated. The concern for enforcing ethics should not result in defamation. At the same time, reporting of known or suspected ethical violations will be encouraged if the reporter is assured of confidentiality. The analogy is to lawyer disciplinary procedures in which there is strict secrecy unless there is a finding that a lawyer acted unethically. Even then, depending on the seriousness of the infraction and surrounding circumstances, the discipline may be only a private reprimand. However, confidentiality protections would not prevent the panel from referring complaints or evidence for possible prosecution.

To the extent that state Sunshine Laws or rights of access to public records are inconsistent with the need for secrecy in the reporting process, they should be amended. No leaks by panel members or staff should be permitted. There is a danger of cover-ups, but the danger is slight. The public should be able to rely on the character of the persons serving on the ethics panel and summary statistics showing number and types of complaints and their disposition. It would be absurd for the ethics enforcement process to be responsible for unwarranted damage to the reputations of public officials.

Another way to encourage reporting is to make failure to report misconduct itself unethical. It may be difficult to prove that someone knew of misconduct but failed to report it. However, that provision will deter participation by other officials in the cover-up of misconduct.

Both the reporting and later communications with the evaluation panel should be treated as conditionally privileged communications. As such, the reporter will not be liable for defamation even if the report is factually incorrect, unless the privilege is abused by reckless or malicious conduct. The conditional privilege will not prevent a reporter who acts in good faith from being sued. However, plaintiffs who sue for defamation based on statements made to the panel during the enforcement process but lose because the conditional privilege applies should be required to pay the defendant's attorneys fees and expenses. That would be a change from the normal rule in American courts, which, unlike those of the English system, do not require the loser to pay the other party's attorney fees.

EVALUATION

Whenever possible, the investigation and evaluation of reported incidents of unethical conduct should be handled by peers of the person whose conduct is questioned. An ethics code adopted and enforced by a cohesive agency or branch of government is the best approach. There should be some procedure for audit or review to ensure that the self-policing is done effectively. Generally, if a legislature or executive agency has had a chance to police itself and has proven unable to do so, the public should insist that an outside body be designated for the task.

Ideally, the procedure for evaluating reports under a departmentwide policy might come before a board of five members, one or two of whom might be managers, with the balance a mixture of other employees. Panel members must be free to act without any pressure from the agency or politicians. A statewide ethics commission should be structured to ensure independence and bipartisanship. Ethics enforcement personnel must not be political appointees.

Confidentiality should be strictly observed. If the accused intentionally publicizes the matter or does so inadvertently while building a defense, the panel is not responsible for the breach of confidentiality. Persons who report suspected unethical conduct are not bound by the secrecy required of panel members and staff. They may wish to complain publicly if they think the panel is covering up misconduct. The risk they take is that the normal rules governing defamation apply, so they will want to be quite sure they are correct.

The enforcement panel must be scrupulously concerned with the rights of the person suspected of misconduct. As a matter of law, due process rights to notice, a fair hearing, and the right to be heard must be observed. After determining that there is probable cause to believe that an infraction of the ethics code has occurred, the person should be informed in detail of the charge and the evidence that appears to support it. He or she should be allowed an adequate time to prepare and seek the help of others, including lawyers, in preparing and presenting a defense. There should be a procedure for appealing the panel's decision within the department or agency. If the action originates in a statewide ethics commission, the only appeal may be to a court.

SANCTIONS

If the code of ethics is formal, part of a statute or the civil service system, sanctions may range from private reprovals to dismissal and damages assessed for injury caused by or money lost as a result of the unethical behavior. Short of expulsion, the most drastic action a congressional ethics committee can take is censure. Only seven senators have been censured in the Senate's history. The most recent censures are those of Senators David Durenberger and Alan Cranston. Durenberger's censure, an action supported by ninety-six senators, was for his knowingly and willfully violating Senate limits on speaking fees and gifts and misleading the Senate in order to be improperly reimbursed. Cranston was censured for peddling his influence to S&L operator Charles Keating.

An informal code will necessarily have less drastic sanctions and will be limited to private warnings to the public employee or official found to have acted improperly, including warnings that can be made part of a personnel file. That difference does not mean that the informal code will be less useful. No employee will find the informal process enjoyable. The value of an enforcement process as a deterrent ought to be substantially the same under either system.

If our premise that most public servants are honest and well meaning is correct, the sanctions for unethical conduct should be extensions of the ethics training and counseling that they should receive. Most reported violations will not be blatant efforts to enrich themselves or criminal conduct but will result from a breakdown in ethics training and awareness. The President's commission quoted Napoleon: "There is no such thing as a bad soldier; there are only poor officers." Egregious violations resulting from intentional conduct are probably also criminal and should be referred for prosecution. The ethics enforcement process itself should resemble continued counseling more than prosecution.

AN ENFORCEMENT MODEL

1. Reporting
   a. All public employees and officials shall report to the ethics panel violations of this code which are observed or reasonably suspected. Failure to make such a report is itself unethical.
   b. All reports to the ethics panel will be kept in the strictest confidence. It is unethical for any panel member or staff person to breach the confidentiality required at every stage of this enforcement process, unless publicity of the matter is part of the sanction imposed. However, the panel may refer complaints or evidence to appropriate authorities for possible investigation or prosecution.
   c. All reports and statements made to the ethics panel by the reporter or witnesses are deemed to be conditionally privileged and cannot be the basis for a claim for defamation unless false and recklessly or maliciously made.
2. The Ethics Panel
   a. The ethics panel will be selected by a method that ensures independence and bipartisanship. When possible, it shall contain peers of the person accused of unethical conduct (the respondent).

b. The respondent shall be notified of and given an opportunity to refute the charge while it is being investigated.

c. After the panel is satisfied that probable cause exists to believe there is substantial basis for the report, the respondent shall be given an adequate time to prepare a response, and a hearing shall be promptly arranged to hear evidence and the respondent's response.

d. The respondent may request the help of any other person(s), including attorneys, for preparation and representation at the hearing.

e. After the hearing, the panel will decide whether the respondent acted unethically and, if so, what sanction is appropriate.

f. Depending on the size and structure of the governmental entity covered by this code of ethics and the severity of the possible sanctions, the respondent may be permitted an appeal to a similar panel within the agency or government or to the courts.

3. Sanctions

a. Ethics codes contained in statutes or ordinances or which are a basis for discipline within the civil service system shall specify the available range of sanctions, from private reprovals to dismissal, and provide guidelines for the imposition of particular sanctions.

b. Violations of informal ethics codes shall be punished by confidential letters or conferences with the ethics panel and/or the agency head or other public official.

c. Because most ethical violations reported under the ethics code will fall short of criminal conduct, the emphasis ought to be on constructive correction, discussing the problem with the public employee or official and helping him see why his action was a mistake or created the appearance of impropriety.

NOTES

1. Recommendation 20, TO SERVE WITH HONOR: THE PRESIDENT'S COMMISSION ON FEDERAL ETHICS LAW REFORM, Mar. 1989, at 92.

2. Recommendation 22, *Id.*

3. Frammolino, *Official Fined for Ethics Conflict*, L.A. Times, Aug. 8, 1991, at B1, col. 6.

4. Ornstein, *Put Congressmen Emeriti on the Ethics Panels*, Wall St. J., May 28, 1991, at A22, col. 3.

5. *Morrison v. Olson*, 487 U.S. 654, 108 S.Ct. 2597, 101 L.Ed. 2d 569 (1988).

6. Recommendation 27, *supra*, note 1.

7. Recommendation 21, *supra*, note 1.

8. *Id.* at 97.

13

Competent or Ethical?

Our conclusion to the study of public service ethics brings us to this false dilemma, a choice between competent public servants or ethical ones. This book disputes the view that *political ethics* is an oxymoron, like *jumbo shrimp* or *military intelligence*. Machiavelli believed that politics was amoral, merely a process of obtaining results through the effective use of power. However, American government is not the best environment for his principles. Our best public servants are idealists who temper their idealism with pragmatism. Machiavellian "realists" become ineffective when they are caught using power illegally or if the public becomes dissatisfied with consistently unethical behavior.

West Virginia Supreme Court Justice Richard Neely believes that voters are more pragmatic than idealistic. He wrote,

What voters really want in a politician is a lying, cheating, corrupt, thieving, wheeling-dealing bastard *who is their friend* and willing to place all his unethical skills entirely at their disposal. Only when such a creature can't be elected does the average voter become enchanted with "honest" government, which simply means that there is no lying, cheating, corrupt, thieving, wheeling-dealing bastard in office who is a friend of the voter's *enemies*.[1]

Perhaps voters will tolerate most unethical behavior. Seventy-five percent of House members charged with ethics violations between 1968 and

1978 were reelected. More recent examples of indicted or convicted politicians reelected without opposition suggest that political effectiveness is more important to the public than ethical awareness. However, we believe there is a slow but steady trend toward public insistence on higher ethical standards for public officials. The existence of well-defined ethics codes will help officials by giving them an excuse to refuse improper requests and avoid improper influences.

A successful code of ethics most be realistic, recognizing that a political system requires compromise and that winning public office often requires an unusual toughness. The Tammany Hall politician George Washington Plunkitt said,

A reformer can't last in politics. He can make a show of it for a while, but he always comes down like a rocket. . . . He hasn't been brought up in the difficult business of politics and he makes a mess of it every time.[2]

If the proposed rules are naive or simplistic, they will be laughingly ignored. The ethical guidelines compiled in the appendix to this book are designed to set high but workable standards. Similar attempts at a comprehensive statement of public service ethics should aim for the same goal.

As we said in the opening chapter, it *is* a fundamental ethical duty to be competent, efficient, and a wise master of public resources. However, critics of a rigorous set of public service ethics believe that tough ethics will drive out good managers. They argue that the best men and women in private life will be reluctant to enter government service because of disclosure requirements or restrictions on their postgovernment activities. They argue that the best career bureaucrats will leave government if a tough ethics code minimizes the perks, the free lunches and junkets, or seems to be harshly judging them in hindsight.

If efficient public servants did leave because stringent ethics were imposed, it would be a hollow victory for ethics. Government does not need white hats on empty heads. Fortunately, there is no evidence that the enforcement of public service ethics would cause such a migration. Even if a few leave government for that reason, there are sufficient numbers of potentially great public servants who are entering government service at this time of heightened sensitivity to ethical issues. They will adjust to a new environment that clearly, emphatically requires higher standards for those in public life.

As more issues of public service ethics become the subject of legislation, officials should not continue to think, as many do now, that if their conduct is legal, it is ethical. The politician who survives an official investigation may claim, "I was exonerated." Usually, that claim merely means that a prosecutor found insufficient evidence to indict but has nothing to do with a declaration that the official acted ethically.

Even where ethics codes acquire the force of law, there will be unforeseen gaps in coverage or ethical dilemmas that the law does not address. For example, a law prohibiting gifts to an official may not explicitly prohibit the gift of expensive vacations or college tuition to the official's close relative. An ethical public servant cannot be satisfied with merely obeying the law. Rather, he or she will instinctively extend the basic principle of honoring the public trust to avoid the appearance of impropriety, as well as impropriety or illegality itself.

President Carter's wish for a government as good as the American people may have been for a less perfect government than he hoped. "We the people" are not always as good or as ethical in daily life as we should be. However, high ethical standards in public service may result in a government as good as the American people should be.

Finally, Americans who are not public officials have ethical duties, also. We should be informed about governmental affairs. We should participate in discussions about government powers and policies, including the proper ethical standards for public officials. We should vote, not only because the outcome of elections is likely to be different, but also because voting leads people to increase their involvement in community affairs. In the 1990 congressional elections only 36.4 percent of the eligible voters voted.[3] Only 63 percent of eligible voters are even registered to vote. We have no right to hold public officials to high ethical standards unless we are willing to act responsibly as citizens.

NOTES

1. Letter from Justice Richard Neely to Richard Wentworth (Apr. 4, 1991).
2. Quoted in B. Jackson, HONEST GRAFT 214 (1988).
3. Gibbs, *Keep the Bums In: Frustrated Voters Send an Angry Message: No to Politics-as-Usual*, TIME, Nov. 19, 1990, 32.

Appendix

A MODEL CODE OF ETHICS FOR PUBLIC OFFICIALS

Premise

Public officials are obligated to render honest judgment, to work hard and efficiently, and to maximize the benefit of government to every citizen. *Public officials* are defined as employees, whether career or appointed, and elected officials at every level of government.

Basic Principles

1. Public officials must not lie, cheat, or steal in any official capacity. They must obey the law. Public officials must always tell the truth to the public, other governmental bodies, and the press, except in extremely limited circumstances, such as war or national emergency, when a temporary deception serves a paramount governmental purpose.

2. Public officials must avoid all conflicts of interest created by business, friendship, or family relationships and must always be careful to avoid even the appearance of impropriety.

3. Public officials owe a fiduciary duty to taxpayers and to all citizens

to ensure that public funds are used efficiently. Officials and all public employees whom they supervise should be as productive as possible.

4. Public officials must not allow zeal for their duties, including such duties as tax collection or law enforcement, to cause them to violate citizens' legal rights. Public servants should not be rude or unresponsive when dealing with the public.

5. Public officials should cooperate with other officials and agencies to maximize the public good, rather than acting out of cronyism or advancing the interests of politicians of a political machine.

6. Public officials should perform their duties based solely on the public good, rather than what is in their best political interests. They should not pressure public employees to assist in the officials' political careers or reelection efforts.

ETHICAL GUIDELINES

Financing Election Campaigns

1. Candidates for public office should divorce themselves as much as possible from the process of raising campaign funds. No candidate should ever pressure contributors by threatening retaliation or the withholding of legitimate governmental action. At a minimum, candidates should expressly state that no donation will cause them, if elected, to take any action that they do not independently believe to be correct. No candidate should permit any campaign staffer or aide to promise or suggest otherwise.

2. Elected officials must ensure that campaign contributors do not receive access to the official or the official's staff that is substantially greater than would be accorded to any constituent. No contributor should receive the benefit of any information that is not publicly known.

3. Candidates and elected officials have a duty to seek fair and equitable campaign financing reform that minimizes the inherent power of incumbents.

4. Candidates should not use personal or family wealth to substantially outspend opponents who rely primarily on contributions, although a reasonable disparity in such spending is justified when the opponent is an incumbent.

5. Candidates should not accept donations from a political party that are made in lieu of a direct donation from an individual, a business, a union, or a PAC if that direct donation would have been a political liability if publicized.

6. Candidates should not accept contributions in either "hard" or "soft" money from individuals, businesses, or unions that are subject to oversight or regulation in which the candidate reasonably expects to be

directly involved. For example, it is an unacceptable conflict of interest for a member of a legislative banking committee to take campaign contributions from the banking industry.

7. Public officials should not have personal PACs. They should not contribute excess campaign funds to other candidates. If an official has a personal PAC, he should not make contributions from it to other candidates or PACs. Public officials who control PACs are guilty of the appearance of impropriety because there is no legitimate reason for such control.

8. Candidates should publicly disclose accurate lists of all contributors and all expenditures as frequently as possible during a campaign, and this disclosure should include the last few days before the election. A final report should be made as soon as possible after the election, in addition to all other reports required by law.

9. Candidates should do everything possible to avoid campaign debt that persists after the election. They should not borrow campaign funds unless there is a reasonable expectation that all loans and bills can be paid with funds raised prior to the election.

10. Candidates should not continue raising campaign funds when it is apparent that a substantial surplus will result.

11. Candidates should return all surplus campaign funds to contributors on a pro rata basis. They should never convert surplus campaign funds to personal use, even if it is legal to do so.

Campaigning

1. Candidates for public office should publicly promise to conduct ethical campaigns, conforming to these standards at a minimum. They should do their best to ensure that campaign staff and supporters will also conduct themselves in an ethical manner and will discipline or dismiss those who do not.

2. Candidates should not permit "dirty tricks" or mean-spirited pranks that confuse or harass opponents. Even in hard-fought campaigns candidates should make every effort to remain personally cordial with opponents and their supporters.

3. Candidates should campaign only on the substance of legitimate issues affecting the electorate. Campaigns should focus more on the positive aspects of the candidate's positions than on the negative aspects of the opponent's views or actions. Facts regarding an opponent's private or family life should never be mentioned, unless there is a legitimate reason that such a fact reflects on the opponent's qualifications for office.

4. Candidates should not make statements that are misleading to reasonable people or rely on issues that are irrelevant to an opponent's qualifications for the office or to the legitimate issues affecting the elec-

torate. This is a definition of unfair campaign tactics. A candidate's staff or supporters may not engage in any campaign tactic that would be unfair if done directly by the candidate.

5. Candidates are under a continuing duty of candor. If they make statements that they believe to be accurate or fair at the time but later learn to have been false or misleading, they should promptly correct such statements or misimpressions. Candidates should try to ensure that corrections are publicized as widely as the original statements.

6. Candidates who feel that they are victims of an unfair campaign tactic should not retaliate in kind. Rather, they should explain to the voters in clear, plain language why the opponent is guilty of unethical conduct and let the voters decide whether their claim is correct.

7. Candidates have a duty to make themselves available to the press and public for open, candid exchanges, subject only to legitimate security concerns. Candidates, whether incumbent or not, who appear only in stage-managed formats unfairly deprive voters of the chance to question them directly.

8. Candidates should seek frequent, public encounters with opponents in which issues can be debated in reasonably unstructured settings. Subject only to generous time limits, candidates should be encouraged to explore issues in detail in debates in which they may be challenged by opponents, the press, and the public.

9. Candidates should not pay money or give anything of value to other politicians in return for an endorsement or a promise not to work against the candidate. Campaigns can pay legitimate out-of-pocket expenses for necessary campaign expenditures, so long as political leaders are not enriched thereby.

10. Candidates should not pay money or give anything of value to a voter directly or to a third party when the candidate knows or suspects that the third party will pay voters.

Elected Officials

1. Elected officials are bound by the same ethical guidelines as those that apply to all public officials and must constantly work to maintain and justify the public trust they have been given.

2. Elected officials must represent all the people in their district, regardless of whether they are voters or whether they supported the official. In addition, officials must act in ways that improve the entire government in which they work, as well as the nation generally.

3. If a candidate for office cannot in good conscience act in ways demanded by a majority of his or her constituents, voters should be clearly informed of that reservation, so they can evaluate the candidate accordingly. If an elected official confronts a conflict between conscience and

the constituents' wishes, the official must act in a principled manner even if it causes political damage to the official.

4. In most matters, legislators should represent the majority view of constituents when it is possible to know that view. Otherwise, legislators should decide issues using their best judgment in light of what best promotes the interests of the constituents and society as a whole.

5. Public officials have a duty to lead public opinion by ensuring that constituents have access to good information and that they have the benefit of the officials' thinking. Officials should attempt to shape public opinion responsibly, rather than merely acting by rote as passive representatives of the public will.

6. Elected officials should be reasonably accessible to the public for the purpose of open debate, discussion, and questioning. Officials should welcome the chance to have open-ended meetings with people at which they can seek public input and explain their own views.

7. Elected officials should be reasonably accessible to the press and media doing interviews, press conferences, and cooperating with all legitimate press inquiries.

8. Elected officials are worthy of the public trust only when they are free from all avoidable conflicts of interest, whether financial, personal, or familial. If there is any doubt about whether a conflict of interest exists, the official should remember the need to avoid even the appearance of impropriety. Decisions made when the official is under an unavoidable conflict of interest should be made publicly and is the result of the official's best judgment.,

9. Elected officials should ensure that influence seekers do not create a conflict of interest or the appearance of impropriety by doing favors for close friends or relatives of the official. If the elected official cannot keep the friend or relative from accepting a gift, contract, or job from a person or business affected by the official's public duties, the official should promptly disclose the relationship.

10. Elected officials should refuse honoraria, speaking fees, or money of any kind from any source that may wish to influence their actions, except for appropriate travel expense reimbursement. However, they should refuse free trips or travel expense reimbursement for junkets or other events at which they do not speak or in cases in which the length or expense of the trip is out of proportion to the legitimate speaking engagement.

11. Elected officials should not hold a major position in a political party.

12. Officials who seek reelection should not solicit political contributions from those who will feel pressured to contribute by reason of the officials' actual or apparent power over them. Elected officials are bound by the ethical duties of all candidates in the raising and spending of campaign funds.

13. Elected officials should not use the privileges of their position to directly aid a reelection campaign. For example, an official who normally sends one newsletter per year to constituents at government expense should not increase the number of such mailings during a reelection year.

14. Public officials should always exercise independent judgment on each issue or decision that comes before them rather than to abdicate that judgment in exchange for the reciprocal promises of other officials.

Appointed Officials

1. Elected officials (appointers) should take all reasonable steps to ensure that appointed officials (appointees) are persons of good character who will be both competent and ethical. Appointers should publicly promise appointees the freedom to act according to their best judgment and without political interference, even when the appointer disagrees.

2. While appointees should demonstrate appropriate loyalty to the appointer, their primary loyalty must be to the public. Assisting the appointer's political agenda is appropriate if the requested action or inaction is otherwise proper and is consistent with the public interest.

3. Appointees should seek public office only for the opportunity to render public service, rather than for personal gain. Appointees should not accept an appointment to public office unless it is clear that they will have the freedom to act ethically without interference or retaliation by the appointer.

4. Appointees should resign from public office if the appointer places them in a situation in which the seriousness of a requested impropriety outweighs the benefit to the public of their continued service. If the impropriety is grossly unethical or criminal, the appointee should resign immediately upon learning of it. If a series of minor improprieties becomes cumulatively serious, the appointee should make it clear to the appointer that those improprieties must stop. If they continue, the appointee should resign.

5. Appointees who seriously disagree with a decision or policy of the appointer may choose to resign as a matter of principle. Appointees may ethically use the same process of balancing the seriousness of the disagreement or importance of the principle with the potential public good that may result if the appointee remains in office.

6. The appointee should resign quietly out of loyalty to the appointer unless the improprieties are individually or cumulatively so serious that the public deserves to know. The former appointee should assist in the effort to correct or prevent the unethical conduct that led to the resignation.

7. Appointees should consider the political nature of most government jobs before accepting an appointment. If they are not comfortable giving

appropriate access or consideration to the appointer's friends or supporters, they should decline the appointment or make their position clear to the appointer.

Civil Servants

1. Public employees who are neither elected nor appointed should be given reasonable job security with dismissal, demotion, or other discipline only for cause or financial exigency. *Cause* includes unethical behavior, including job-related violations of law or breaches of a code of ethics adopted by the relevant office or agency. Employees should not be adversely affected because of ethical conduct that does not serve the political interests of a supervisor or official.

2. Agency executives and politicians should protect the interests of public employees by aggressively seeking fair pay and working conditions and by shielding employees from direct or indirect political pressure.

3. Government should seek to recognize and reward outstanding employees in nonmonetary ways as well, including public rewards and incentives.

4. Officials with patronage power over employees outside the civil service system should treat the employees as if civil service protections applied and encouraged ethical conduct regardless of political consequences.

5. Career public employees should abstain from public political activity such as campaigning or fund raising, although they should vote and be involved in civic or nonpartisan community roles.

6. A Model Code of Ethics for Public Employees:

    a. Duties Owed to Citizens

       —Every citizen with whom I deal should be treated with the same courtesy and respect that I would want if our roles were reversed.

       —I will not treat citizens differently because of their race, national origin, religion, sex, age, or political beliefs.

       —I will not engage in any action, such as a strike or slowdown, that endangers public health or safety. I will not engage in any such action unless all other attempts to resolve legitimate grievances about pay or working conditions have failed.

    b. Duties Owed to Taxpayers

       —I will work productively, efficiently, and honestly. I will look for ways to improve my own performance and that of my office because the goal of greater productivity is increased government services or lower taxes.

       —I will not accept bribes or gifts, however small, that are given to me because of my public employment or with an intention to influence decisions made in my work.

—I will scrupulously avoid all conflicts of interest and will be sensitive to avoid even the appearance of impropriety.

c. Duties Owed to Other Agencies and Public Employees
—I will work closely with other agencies and their employees in an effort to help all of government be as productive as possible.

—I will share relevant information, ideas, and resources without being primarily concerned about interdepartmental politics.

d. Duties Owed to Agency Executives and Politicians
—I will treat my managers with the same respect and courtesy that I expect to receive as an employee.

—I will refuse to treat any customer more or less favorably than I would otherwise treat them or to compromise my job performance in any way because doing so would advance the political interests of a supervisor or agency head.

—If I know of or reasonably suspect impropriety within government or my agency, including misconduct by my manager(s), I will notify the appropriate governmental authority so that the impropriety can be remedied. If reporting through channels would be futile or if the misconduct is ignored, I will contact the appropriate officials in other agencies or branches of government. Only if that does not result in a proper response to the impropriety will I inform the public or the media directly. All my actions in this regard will be thoughtful and responsible, rather than publicity seeking, but I will undertake them even though I may suffer personally as a result.

Lobbyists

1. Lobbyists should be viewed as one resource available to public officials for information and ideas about public business.

2. Public officials should not vote or take other action solely on the advice or request of lobbyists but should always apply independent judgment to their duties based on all available information, including that supplied by lobbyists.

3. Public officials should not accept meals, drinks, or gifts, however labeled, from lobbyists. Speaking fees or honoraria in excess of legitimate travel expenses should be refused. Large social or seminar functions may be attended because no undue influence on the official is likely to result.

4. Lobbyists should not receive access to a public official or the official's staff that competing lobbyists or any citizen would not also receive. Public officials should be especially cautious about dealing with lobbyists who are former employees or associates because of the appearance of impropriety. While it is natural to give preference to trusted sources of advice or information, officials should never appear to be heavily influenced by particular lobbyists.

5. Consistent with other ethical considerations about campaign financing, public officials should distance themselves from lobbyist-directed contributions and clearly communicate to contributors and their own staff that such contributions will not result in special access or considerations of the contributors' interests that are significantly different from access or consideration accorded to noncontributors.

6. Public officials should refuse campaign contributions from lobbyists or their employers that are proffered near the time of a requested vote or action or during a time when the lobbyists' interests are receiving unusual legislative or governmental attention.

7. Public officials should support and implement stringent reporting and disclosure laws on both lobbyists and public officials so that the public can evaluate relationships between them. Such laws should have stiff penalties and sure enforcement mechanisms.

Paying Public Servants

1. The public owes a duty to public employees at all levels of government to provide adequate pay, benefits, and working conditions. Elected officials and agency officials should work effectively with the public and the legislatures to ensure the public employees are fairly compensated, even if fair pay is not politically popular.

2. Full-time public officials should not receive income from outside activities, other than passive income from investments or businesses in which they have an ownership interest but do not actively manage.

3. Full-time public officials should not serve on the board of directors of a for-profit corporation or receive pay for serving on the board of a nonprofit corporation. Unpaid service on a nonprofit corporation's board should be limited so that there is no interference with the officials' public duties.

4. Part-time public officials who are expected to maintain other full-time employment must avoid all conflicts of interest, as well as the appearance of conflicts, between the full-time job and their public duties.

5. All public officials should fully disclose all sources and amounts of outside income, although the names of professional clients may be replaced with specific client categories if disclosure would violate confidentiality.

6. Public officials who own investments or businesses that pose conflicts of interest should sell those assets. If it is impractical or unfair to require divestiture, those assets should be placed in a blind trust over which the trustee has complete control, with minimal reporting to the official. If the official insists on placing conditions on the trustee's power, such conditions should be made public, but in no event should the official continue to actively manage the asset. No blind trust is required if the

holdings are so small that disclosure by itself will minimize the appearance of impropriety.

7. Public officials should refuse all speaking fees or honoraria from companies or industries that might be seeking influence over them, although they may accept reimbursement for travel expenses if such reimbursement is publicly disclosed.

8. Public officials should refuse all gifts, however characterized, except for gifts from civic groups that seek no influence on the official and ceremonial gifts between government officials. Any gift accepted by an official is public property and should be reported and turned over to the government.

9. Public officials should attempt to keep close friends or relatives of the official from accepting gifts or favors from persons or companies affected by the officials' public duties. If the elected official cannot prevent the acceptance of a gift or favor that has the appearance of impropriety, the official should promptly disclose that such a gift was made in order to dispel the improper appearance.

10. Elected officials should make complete disclosure of all financial, business, and personal dealings so that the public can evaluate whether the official is influenced by a conflict of interest. The disclosure should be wide-ranging and almost certainly more than may be required by law.

The Revolving Door

1. Public officials should only seek or retain their positions based on a proper motive to serve the legitimate ends of government, rather than to accumulate excessive personal wealth or influence.

2. Persons may enter government service intending to stay for only a limited period of time in order to gain a greater knowledge of government generally or of a particular agency *or* to lend their expertise at higher levels within government. In any case, they should commit themselves to a reasonable period of time in that position, so that wasteful turnover is minimized and they can make a meaningful contribution to government service.

3. Employees leaving private industry for government service should refuse any severance benefits or "golden handshakes" that were not earned during the private employment.

4. Public officials who leave government service should not seek employment or clients with any promise, express or implied, that they have informal access or influence because of their prior experience. They should not take advantage of the access or influence that they do have to obtain information or action for themselves, private employers, or clients to which others are not equally entitled.

5. Former public officials should not use information obtained in government service that was not available to the public at the time.

6. Public officials should treat former colleagues who are now in the private sector on the same terms as any other person with whom the official deals. Officials should be aware that there is an appearance of impropriety from any informality or cooperation accorded to former colleagues, even if others would have been treated equally.

Lawyers as Public Officials

1. Lawyers who are also public officials should comply with standards of public service ethics, as well as codes of legal ethics. They must be especially sensitive to avoid the appearance of impropriety.

2. While it is permissible to represent clients attracted to a lawyer-official because of the official's public service, clients must be told that no influence on public business will be permitted and that if a specific conflict of interest develops, the client must seek new representation.

3. Prosecutors are bound by standards of public service ethics, as well as codes of legal ethics, and should exercise their discretion and power over people objectively without regard to political considerations.

4. Judges should strictly comply with the Code of Judicial Conduct and absolutely avoid the appearance of impropriety. If their office is elective, they should refuse all campaign contributions from parties or lawyers in pending cases, as well as any contribution intended to buy influence over future cases.

The Private Lives of Public Officials

1. Only those private indiscretions or family problems which might reasonably affect the public official's job performance should be publicly disclosed. If the official does not voluntarily disclose those relevant public matters, the media or other citizens have a duty to investigate and report them.

2. The public has a right to know about a public official's serious illness or injury. Candidates for major full-time public offices should disclose serious health problems before seeking election or appointment.

3. Public officials should arrange personal financial affairs so that job performance is not impaired and possible conflicts of interest are minimized. Wealthy full-time officials should create blind trusts that free them from all concern for preserving their wealth.

4. Public officials should lead exemplary personal lives in order to avoid the appearance of impropriety. The public has a right to know about private moral failures that suggest character defects or conflicts of interest that may affect the official's judgment or job performance.

Enforcing Public Service Ethics

1. Reporting

   a. All public employees and officials shall report to the ethics panel violations
      of this code which are observed or reasonably suspected. Failure to
      make such a report is itself unethical.

   b. All reports to the ethics panel will be kept in the strictest confidence. It is
      unethical for any panel member or staff person to breach the confiden-
      tiality required at every stage of this enforcement process, unless pub-
      licity of the matter is part of the sanction imposed. However, the panel
      may refer complaints or evidence to appropriate authorities for possible
      investigation or prosecution.

   c. All reports and statements made to the ethics panel by the reporter or
      witnesses are deemed to be conditionally privileged and cannot be the
      basis for a claim for defamation unless false and recklessly or maliciously
      made.

2. The Ethics Panel

   a. The ethics panel will be selected by a method that ensures independence
      and bipartisanship. When possible, it shall contain peers of the person
      accused of unethical conduct (the respondent).

   b. The respondent shall be notified of and given an opportunity to refute the
      charge while it is being investigated.

   c. After the panel is satisfied that probable cause exists to believe there is a
      substantial basis for the report, the respondent shall be given an adequate
      time to prepare a response, and a hearing shall be promptly arranged to
      hear evidence and the respondent's response.

   d. The respondent may request the help of any other person(s), including
      attorneys, for preparation and representation at the hearing.

   e. After the hearing, the panel will decide whether the respondent acted uneth-
      ically and, if so, what sanction is appropriate.

   f. Depending on the size and structure of the governmental entity covered by
      this code of ethics and the severity of the possible sanctions, the re-
      spondent may be permitted an appeal to a similar panel within the agency
      or government or to the courts.

3. Sanctions

   a. Ethics codes contained in statutes or ordinances or which are a basis for
      discipline within the civil service system shall specify the available range
      of sanctions, from private reprovals to dismissal, and provide guidelines
      for the imposition of particular sanctions.

   b. Violations of informal ethics codes shall be punished by confidential letters
      or conferences with the ethics panel and/or the agency head or other
      public official.

c. Because most ethical violations reported under the ethics code will fall far short of criminal conduct, the emphasis ought to be on constructive correction, discussing the problem with the public employee or official so that they will see why the action was a mistake or created the appearance of impropriety.

Selected Bibliography

Baker, Daniel B., ed. POLITICAL QUOTATIONS. Detroit: Gale Research, 1990.

Bell, Griffin B., and Ronald J. Ostrow. TAKING CARE OF THE LAW. Atlanta: Mercer University Press, 1989.

Birnbaum, Jeffrey H., and Alan S. Murray. SHOWDOWN AT GUCCI GULCH: LAWMAKERS, LOBBYISTS, AND THE UNLIKELY TRIUMPH OF TAX REFORM. New York: Alfred A. Knopf, 1988.

Jackson, Brooks. HONEST GRAFT: BIG MONEY AND THE AMERICAN POLITICAL PROCESS. New York: Alfred A. Knopf, 1988.

Lieber, Francis. MANUAL OF POLITICS. 1838.

Noona, John. BRIBES. New York: Macmillan, 1984.

REPORT OF THE PRESIDENT'S COMMISSION ON FEDERAL ETHICS LAW REFORM. Washington, D.C.: U.S. Government Printing Office, Mar. 1989.

Ryn, Claes G. DEMOCRACY AND THE ETHICAL LIFE: A PHILOSOPHY OF POLITICS AND COMMUNITY. 2d ed. Washington, D.C.: Catholic University of America Press, 1990.

Stern, Phillip M. THE BEST CONGRESS MONEY CAN BUY. New York: Alfred A. Knopf, 1988.

Thompson, Dennis F. POLITICAL ETHICS AND PUBLIC OFFICE. Cambridge, Mass.: Harvard University Press, 1987.

Vance, Mary. POLITICAL ETHICS: A BIBLIOGRAPHY. Monticello, Ill.: Vance Bibliographies, 1982.

Index

ABOUT THE AUTHORS

W. J. MICHAEL CODY practices law in Memphis, Tennessee, as a senior partner in the firm of Burch, Porter & Johnson. He was formerly a member of the Memphis City Council, a candidate for Mayor of Memphis, and U.S. Attorney General for the state of Tennessee. Mr. Cody coordinated Jimmy Carter's 1976 presidential campaign in Tennessee and has been active in legal ethics and reform efforts.

RICHARDSON R. LYNN is a Professor of Law at the Pepperdine University School of Law in Malibu, California. In addition to teaching at various law schools, he served as Professor of Business Law and Ethics at the Jack C. Massey Graduate School of Business in Nashville.